THE TWELVE KEYS
LEADERS' GUIDE

BOOKS BY
KENNON L. CALLAHAN, PH.D.

———

TWELVE KEYS LEADERS' GUIDE

An Approach for Grassroots, Key Leaders, and Pastors Together

Kennon L. Callahan

JOSSEY-BASS
A Wiley Imprint
www.josseybass.com

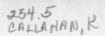
Published by Jossey-Bass
A Wiley Imprint
989 Market Street, San Francisco, CA 94103-1741—www.josseybass.com

Readers should be aware that Internet Web sites offered as citations and/or sources for further information may have changed or disappeared between the time this was written and when it is read.

Limit of Liability/Disclaimer of Warranty: While the publisher and author have used their best efforts in preparing this book, they make no representations or warranties with respect to the accuracy or completeness of the contents of this book and specifically disclaim any implied warranties of merchantability or fitness for a particular purpose. No warranty may be created or extended by sales representatives or written sales materials. The advice and strategies contained herein may not be suitable for your situation. You should consult with a professional where appropriate. Neither the publisher nor author shall be liable for any loss of profit or any other commercial damages, including but not limited to special, incidental, consequential, or other damages.

Jossey-Bass books and products are available through most bookstores. To contact Jossey-Bass directly call our Customer Care Department within the U.S. at 800-956-7739, outside the U.S. at 317-572-3986, or fax 317-572-4002.

Jossey-Bass also publishes its books in a variety of electronic formats. Some content that appears in print may not be available in electronic books.

Library of Congress Cataloging-in-Publication Data
Callahan, Kennon L.
  The twelve keys leaders' guide : an approach for grassroots, key leaders, and pastors together/Kennon L. Callahan. — 2nd ed.
       p. cm.
  Includes index.
  Rev. ed. of: Twelve keys to an effective church. The leaders' guide.
  ISBN 978-0-470-55928-4 (cloth)
  1. Church renewal. 2. Christian leadership. I. Callahan, Kennon L.
Twelve keys to an effective church. The leaders' guide. II. Title.
  BV600.3.C34 2010
  254'.5—dc22
                                                            2009038857

Printed in the United States of America
SECOND EDITION
HB Printing   10 9 8 7 6 5 4 3 2 1

CONTENTS

This work is dedicated to Ken and Mike.

God blesses Julie and me with wonderful gifts.
    We are amazed at God's generosity with us.
        We are blessed with two remarkable sons.
            Kennon L. Callahan Jr.
            Michael Thomas Callahan

All parents hope their children turn out well.
    Our sons have turned out better than one could have hoped.
        Their compassion and wisdom,
            their creativity and leadership,
                their judgment and common sense,
                    their spirit of grace and generosity
                    are extraordinary.

We are grateful for who they are and for their contributions in the lives of many persons.
May God continue to bless them with peace and grace.

                        Kennon L. Callahan, Ph.D.

A Prayer

Living God, we are grateful for the generous grace
with which you bless our lives.
  We are thankful you encourage us
  to claim our strengths.
    We are amazed at how you run to us
    with your compassion.

We give thanks for how you act swiftly in our lives.
  Your grace pours forth like the rushing spring rivers.
    Your hope stirs like a promising summer sunrise.

Help us, Living God, to live whole, healthy lives
in your grace.
  Grant us peace and hope, this day,
  and throughout our lives.
    May our lives count well for your mission.

Surround us with your grace.
  Sustain us with your peace.
    Lead us with your hope.

                                        Amen.

                        Kennon L. Callahan, Ph.D.

A BIRD ON THE WING

MT. PRINCETON

I am writing to you from our home on Mt. Princeton. The mountain is 14,197 feet high. There are fifteen mountains in the area, all above 14,000 feet. It is among the most beautiful regions in the world.

Our home is at 9,000 feet. My study is on the upper story of our home. As I look out my window to the east, I see the sun rising, its gentle rays lighting the top of the mountain with a quiet rose salmon glow. From the south windows of my study, I see the sweep of trees that cover this area of the mountain.

I have written seventeen of my eighteen books on Mt. Princeton. This is the eighteenth. The peace and quiet, the grandeur and strength of the mountain, and of the mountains around, gives one a sense of the majesty and the glory of the grace of God.

We have been blessed with many friends coming to visit us . . . . from across the world.

We have enjoyed friends from Australia, New Zealand, Canada, South Africa, England, and all parts of the United States. We are grateful for our wonderful times together on Mt. Princeton. We have enjoyed wondrous outings in the mountains, much laughter and good fun, deep conversations, and the closeness of being friends and family together.

We have a few neighbors. They are good neighbors . . . . the best of neighbors. Mostly, we enjoy the stillness and silence, the beauty and splendor, the serenity and solitude. It is a wonderful place to live . . . . and to write.

DAD AND MOM

Dad passed away on February 2, 2008. He lived ninety-six years and four months. We are grateful for his love and compassion, his wisdom and common sense, his gentle humor and his good spirits. He was clear of mind and a blessing to everyone, right up to his passing on.

Toward the end, amidst the difficulties and doctors, the trips and treatments, his spirit of grace and good humor, his deep interest in the people who were helping him, continued to encourage all of us.

Julie and I have had the privilege of sharing with him and helping him during these past years. He has been of thoughtful help with us as well. We are grateful we could be of help with him. We miss his wisdom, his gentle laughter, his kindness, and his spirit of confidence and assurance.

Dad and Mom moved to be near us in 1991. We have shared many, many good times together. Mom passed away on December 19, 2001. In her later years, we devoted much time to being of help with her. She was eighty-seven years of age when she passed away. Mom and Dad had been married for sixty-eight years. They were married on Palm Sunday, April 9, 1933, at the First Methodist Church in Cuyahoga Falls, Ohio. We are grateful for our years with her.

This book might have appeared sooner had we not devoted so much time, in recent years, with Dad and Mom. It is a richer and deeper book for our years of sharing and caring with Dad and with Mom. We have a clearer sense of what is genuinely important in life, of what is precious and central. We are grateful for our many conversations with them. Their understanding of what counts in this life's pilgrimage has been most helpful.

Their spirit of grace, their love for one another, their years of wisdom and discernment, and their love and compassion have contributed deeply and richly to this work. It is a more helpful book for their contributions. We hope there are persons in your life who bless you in the countless ways my father and mother continue to bless us. We hope this book blesses your life and your congregation.

JULIE AND THE STARS

Miss Leavitt's Stars, The Untold Story of the Woman Who Discovered How to Measure the Universe is a wonderful book by George Johnson, a grand tribute to an extraordinary person. Henrietta Swan Leavitt did her research at the Harvard Observatory nearly a century ago. On page 54 of Johnson's memorable book, we discover these words:

> In the late 1700s the elder Herschel, William, discovered that stars in the direction of the constellation Hercules move according to a peculiar pattern: over the years, they seem to be fanning out from a distant point, as snow flakes seem to do when viewed in the headlights of a car speeding through the night. In the opposite direction, back toward the constellation Columba, the stars converge, like snowflakes seen from the rear window.
>
> Our solar system, he concluded, was leaving Columba and heading toward Hercules. Astronomers have since clocked the speed of this journey through the galaxy at about 12 miles per second, or more than 30 million miles a year . . . . The ancient Greeks were looking at a slightly different sky.

Our Milky Way galaxy is soaring through the universe at extraordinary speed.

We met in our high school. Julie was in the tenth grade. I was in the twelfth grade. During second period, her study hall was on the third floor, room 315. My study hall was on the second floor, the large library, room 202.

I was on the Varsity Debate Team.

My speech coach, Mr. Heinz, mentored Julie's study hall in room 315. I would secure a pass to visit with him so we could discuss the strategies for the coming debates, especially those on the weekend ahead. Julie sat in the front row, near Mr. Heinz's desk. I can see her sitting there now, as I write this. We shared conversations together.

We became friends. She invited me to a square dance at her church. We had a good time. We enjoyed being together. We dated. We dated again. We fell in love. We decided to go steady. Time passed. We became engaged. Time passed. We married. On August 11, 2009, we celebrated sharing fifty-three wonderful years of marriage together.

In the span of these fifty-three years, our galaxy system has traveled 1,590,000,000 million miles closer to the constellation Hercules. For Julie and me, it is an amazing trip through the stars.

In quilting circles, particularly in the area of our home on Mt. Princeton in Colorado, Julie is well known. Better known than I am. I meet someone new in the area. With considerable delight and appreciation, the person says, "Oh, you're Julie's husband!" Amidst the degrees and honors, books and seminars, accolades and awards, the highest honor I have is to be known as "Julie's husband."

She is a remarkable person. The most remarkable person I know. Her love and compassion, her wisdom and kindness, her common sense and thoughtfulness are amazing gifts to all with whom she associates. We share a wonderful pilgrimage together.

A BIRD ON THE WING

A distinguished theologian was giving a major lectureship, near the end of the theologian's life. People had gathered from across the planet in tribute and to learn. It was a grand time.

After presenting his lecture, the theologian welcomed questions. A theology student raised his hand and said, "Professor, can you tell me what you mean by this passage in one of your early books?" The student read the passage. The professor said to the student, "Did I write that?" The student responded, "Yes, it is right here on this page in your book."

The distinguished professor responded, "Oh, my good friend, theology is a bird on the wing. I have moved well beyond that."

I agree. Some ideas have lasting value. Some ideas are a bird on the wing. In this book, you will discover some matters of lasting value, and much that is new.

God Bless You.

THE TWELVE KEYS
LEADERS' GUIDE

Part One

MOMENTUM

MOTIVATIONS

MOMENTUM

Momentum, resources, and strengths create strong, healthy congregations.

Five qualities contribute to a congregation having momentum . . . . having a strong track record of action, implementation, and momentum.

Momentum begins with a motivational match.
Momentum grows as persons achieve key objectives.
Momentum develops power with an effective long-range plan.
Momentum moves forward as we discover the value of excellent mistakes and as we recognize that some objectives are worth not doing.
Momentum deepens as we value memory, change, conflict, and hope.

Without these qualities, congregations do not have a strong track record. Regrettably, some congregations have become preoccupied with meetings and coordination, indecision and analysis paralysis, inertia and impassivity, despair, depression, and despondency.

As you help your congregation, think through which of these five qualities are already present and which ones you can grow forward as you move toward your congregation's future. This chapter and the remaining chapters on momentum discuss these qualities in depth.

MOTIVATIONS

Momentum begins with motivation. Motivations stir momentum. Strong, healthy congregations create a motivational match.

The major motivations present in people and in congregations are:

Compassion
Community
Hope
Challenge
Reasonability
Commitment

Frequently, I refer to these as motivational resources. Motivation is internal, not external. These are the constructive motivational resources inside a person with which persons motivates themselves forward.

All six are present in every person. God blesses every person with all six. You can grow any of the motivations forward in your life. For a variety of reasons, people tend to have grown forward one or two as their primary motivations for this time of life. Life is a pilgrimage. Life is a search. At another stage of life, you might grow forward another of the motivational resources.

The primary motivational resources influence how (and whether) people give their strengths, gifts, and competencies to the life and mission of the congregation.

Compassion has to do with sharing, caring, giving of one's self, and supporting. Many people do what they do in life and in their congregation out of the spirit of compassion.

Community has to do with good fun, good times, fellowship, affiliation, belonging, and the sense of family and home. Many people do what they do in a congregation out of this sense of roots, place, and belonging.

Challenge has to do with accomplishment, achievement, and attainment. Some people rise to the bait of an excellent challenge. They thrive on accomplishing things that others claim cannot be done. Some people do what they do in the congregation out of this sense of challenge, accomplishment, and achievement.

Reasonability has to do with data, analysis, logic, thinking, and "it makes good sense." Some people do what they do in life and in their congregation out of this sense of reasonability.

Commitment has to do with dedication. Some people do what they do in life and in a congregation out of a sense of duty, vow, obligation, loyalty, and faithfulness. They have a deep commitment to the congregation's surviving, thriving, and well-being. They have a commitment to the congregation's work and mission.

All of these motivational resources are present in a given congregation. Two of the six are predominant among the key leaders. Two are predominant among the grassroots. Two are predominant in the pastor (and staff). Two tend to predominate among many of the unchurched in the community. These distinctive motivational configurations constitute the motivational map of a congregation.

A MOTIVATIONAL MATCH

I am with many congregations who say to me, "Dr. Callahan, we want you to know our worship attendance is strong, many people attend, many people do most of the work, and many people give generously." I immediately know I am with congregations who have a motivational match.

Congregations with a strong track record of action, implementation, and momentum have an excellent match of motivational resources between key leaders, the pastor (and staff), the grassroots in the congregation, and the unchurched in the community.

The motivational match happens whenever the key leaders, grassroots, pastor and staff, and unchurched find a motivational

match . . . . a common motivational resonance with two of
these three:

Compassion
Community
Hope

We do not need resonance on all three. We will have strong
momentum when we have a match on any two. A match occurs

A Motivational Match in Strong, Healthy Congregations

	Key Leaders	Grassroots	Pastor Staff	UnChurched
Compassion	●	●	●	●
Community	●	●	●	●
Hope				
Challenge				
Reasonability				
Commitment				

Compassion: sharing, caring, giving, loving, serving   Challenge: accomplishment, achievement, attainment
Community: good fun, good times, belonging, family   Reasonability: data, analysis, logic, it makes good sense
Hope: confidence, assurance in the grace of God   Commitment: duty, vow, obligation, loyalty

A Motivational Gap: Weak, Declining and Dying Congregations

	Key Leaders	Grassroots	Pastor Staff	UnChurched
Compassion		●		●
Community		●		●
Hope				
Challenge	●		●	
Reasonability				
Commitment	●		●	

when two of these are the prevailing motivational resources in the congregation. There is a strong sense of continuity, reliability, and stability in the congregation. There is a healthy spirit of momentum. We act swiftly.

A strong, healthy congregation develops a motivational match between the key leaders, the grassroots, the pastor and staff, and the unchurched. A weak, declining congregation creates a motivational gap. A dying congregation makes the motivational gap wider.

A MOTIVATIONAL GAP

I am with many congregations who say to me, "Dr. Callahan, we want you to know our worship attendance is meager, the same few people attend, the same few people do most of the work, and the same few people give most of the money." I immediately know I am with congregations who have a motivational gap. Wherever there is a mismatch of motivational resources, there is a weak or nonexistent track record of implementation.

I share this suggestion with both the key leaders and the pastor: "You want to bridge from your predominant motivational resources to those that are present among the grassroots. Then, you will motivate and mobilize the strengths, gifts, competencies, and financial resources of the grassroots."

The way forward is to **bridge** the motivational resources to create a helpful match.

Frequently, the reason some things do not happen in a local congregation is because what motivates the key leaders and the pastor differs from what motivates the grassroots of the congregation, and does not resonate with the unchurched. The keys leaders and the pastor share the same motivational resources, but the grassroots motivate themselves out of different motivational resources. They do not resonate well . . . . fit well together.

There is a "motivational gap." Note . . . . it is not a commitment gap. Sometimes, that is what pastors and key leaders mistakenly conclude, particularly as they tend to work out of the motivational resource of commitment.

In a motivational gap, the key leaders and pastor broad-cast on the radio wavelengths of challenge and commitment. The grassroots and the unchurched have their radios tuned to compassion and community. There is no resonance. There is no match. It is a motivational gap.

In committee meeting after committee meeting, the key leaders and the pastor say to one another, "If people were only more committed and would rise to the challenge, this bloom-ing venture would get better." The hook, the catch is that the grassroots and the unchurched do not motivate themselves in high challenge, deeply committed ways.

Regrettably, high challenged, deeply committed keys leaders look for pastors who look like them. They create a wider moti-vational gap. In this situation, I gently suggest to the key leaders and the pastor, "Good friends, your *challenge* is to develop a strong *commitment* to doing what you do out of the two motiva-tional resources of *compassion* and *community*." This is the *reasonable* thing you can do . . . . focus on the motivational resources of compassion and community." This is a motivational *bridge*.

I will ask key leaders whether they have grandchildren. They do. They have pictures. They joyfully share their delight. They speak of all the good fun things they do with their grandchildren. They say, "If we knew how much fun grandchildren were going to be, we would have had them first."

I suggest to them that they live the motivations of com-passion and community with their grandchildren. These are the motivations present in their grandchildren. I suggest they will do well when they relate to the grassroots the same way they relate to their grandchildren. It is a motivational *bridge*.

MOTIVATING GRASSROOTS MEMBERS

It happens again and again in congregations. People say to me, "Dr. Callahan, there are only a few of us who do everything." This happens because of a motivational gap. Often, the faithful few are motivated by commitment. Thus, the leadership recruitment is pitched toward commitment. The grassroots members do not respond to commitment. They respond best to compassion or community.

In thinking through how to raise funds for a fellowship hall and church school facilities, you can design a giving campaign to appeal to the persons who you hope will be generous givers. Do you want to raise the money primarily with the key leaders? Do you want to raise the money primarily with the grassroots?

I once asked each person on the finance committee to list these six motivational resources on a sheet of paper. I invited each of them to think which two motivational resources influence the grassroots of their congregation. I reminded them not to think about leaders but rather the grassroots. Independently and individually, each person of the finance committee checked "compassion" and "community" as the major motivational resources influencing the grassroots.

I said to them, "The best thing you can do is to launch the giving campaign with the best good-fun, good-times fellowship, community-oriented, family reunion supper this congregation has ever seen. In the brochure, do not focus on the square footage of the buildings. Instead, you can show *people pictures* of who will benefit from the new facilities. Describe the mission and programs that will take place in the new facilities. Share how the new facilities will help advance forward person's lives and destinies in compassionate, community ways. Share how people will discover the grace of God."

These key leaders motivate themselves primarily by challenge and commitment. They wanted to raise the money primarily from the grassroots. They remembered their grandchildren. They remembered what I had suggested. They decided *not* to launch the campaign with a Loyalty Sunday that appealed to commitment. They decided *not* to have a "challenge thermometer goal" of a specific dollar amount that *must* be reached in order to do this project. They decided not to remind people of their "commitment vows."

They had done all of these things in previous campaigns. They had usually "fallen short." The giving had come mostly from key leaders. Little came from the grassroots.

I had told the finance committee, "If you prefer to raise the money from among *only* the key leaders in this congregation, be sure to focus on the motivations of challenge and commitment. You will raise the money primarily from among the key leaders. This is what you have taught me about your previous campaigns. The lesson to learn is to focus on the motivational resources prevalent among the grassroots if you hope to raise the money with the grassroots.

In weak and declining and dying congregations, I find many of the key leaders originally became part of the congregation out of the motivations of compassion and community. But, over the past twenty-five years, the few remaining key leaders have changed the focus of their motivations to challenge and commitment. To be sure, the only people left are those people who are committed to the challenge of trying to keep this congregation going so that it might minimally survive.

I find reasonability a major motivation in communities that have a high density of engineers, scientists, and data processing persons. In small college towns, with a high density of professors, reasonability will be a major motivation.

Sometimes, I discover a congregation that has been badly burned by several traumatic events in recent years. In this setting, the key leaders learn the motivation of reasonability. Understandably, people in this situation will hesitate—want to make sure a plan makes good sense—before they put their hand into the flame yet another time. The last few times they did, they got burned.

Now, I have never yet met a couple who got married out of the motivation of reasonability. If it made reasonable sense, most people would not be married. People get married out of compassion, community, and hope. Then, they rationalize why it made sense to get married earlier rather than later.

An overworked motivation is commitment. Someone says to me, "Dr. Callahan, what we need in our congregation is more commitment." My response is "Good friend, you have just taught me you are a long-time Christian. The early motivations that draw all of us to the Christian life are compassion, community, and hope. Then, over twenty or more years, some grow forward the motivation of commitment."

I add, "If there were lots of longtime Christians out there, we would do well on commitment. What are out there are persons who are unchurched . . . . who are on the verge of beginning their early years in a Christian life."

I go on to suggest, "You have taught me that a major motivation out of which you do what you do is commitment. But, good friend, many persons do what they do in the congregation out of compassion, community, hope, challenge, or reasonability. You are wanting people to motivate themselves the way you motivate yourself. You will do better when you focus on the actual way people motivate themselves."

Some key leaders and pastors, with a primary motivation of commitment, press the congregation to "remember their membership vows." For persons for whom *compassion* is their primary motivation, the phrase "remember your membership vows" may end up sounding like "remember to clean up your room."

To be sure, the membership vows of many denominations were written by people whose primary motivation was commitment. They were longtime Christians when they wrote the vows. The early vows are more like, "Will you love the Lord your God with all your heart, and mind, and soul, and strength? Will you love your neighbor as you love yourself?"

In some congregations, it would be helpful during giving campaigns to have compassion cards rather than commitment cards. It would make better sense to have a Love Sunday rather than a Loyalty Sunday. It would be more helpful to have a Community Sunday rather than a Commitment Sunday.

COMPETENCIES AND COMMITMENT

Most ministers are competent as ministers. It is not true that all ministers are incompetent. It is not true that only some ministers are incompetent. It is true that some people are incompetent as ministers. That does not mean they are incompetent. It means simply that they are incompetent only for the position of minister.

Shortstops are competent as shortstops. It is not true that shortstops are incompetent. It is true that some people who are competent as shortstops are incompetent as pitchers. Some persons do not have the competencies for some positions. They do have the competencies for other positions.

Some people who are incompetent as ministers use the bludgeon of commitment to excuse their own ineptness. As a matter of fact, the ploy of charging people with lack of commitment is often an effort at guilt transference. Some people are aware of their own ineptness and incompetence as ministers but try to transfer guilt to the members by using the push for commitment.

When things don't go well, some ministers blame the grassroots for a lack of commitment. In fact, the problem may be their lack of specific competencies. They miss the fact that the grassroots motivate themselves on compassion, community, or hope. To miss this is evidence that one is incompetent. Sometimes, a declining worship attendance is due to the lack of a preaching competency. Some few ministers, rather than working on their preaching, fall back on blaming the grassroots for a lack of commitment.

Some ministers preach sermons on commitment that are really sermons of displaced anger, dumped on a congregation. You are welcome to preach a sermon on commitment. Do it with a spirit of compassion. It will be a helpful sermon.

Preaching, however stumbling and inept, which focuses on the motivations of compassion, community, and hope will go further than the preaching which pulverizes people for their lack of commitment. It is regrettable that commitment has become an overworked motivation resource in many congregations. Further, it is regrettable that inept, incompetent persons use the excuse of lack of commitment as their way to divert responsibility. Commitment and compassion are good friends in strong, healthy congregations.

COMPASSION AND COMMUNITY

Many, many unchurched persons are attracted to congregations that share a sense of compassion and community rather than a sense of commitment. Commitment is a motivational resource developed among "longtime Christians." What draws and attracts new people to a congregation is their search for compassion . . . . sharing and caring in which they can participate. What draws people to a congregation is their search for community . . . . roots, place, belonging. What draws people to a congregation is their longing for hope. New people are frequently drawn to a congregation by the major motivations of compassion, community, and hope.

One new congregation mailed out a brochure in its community. The cover of the brochure read, "Come, join in the challenge of starting a new (*denominational name*) church." The brochure focused on and appealed to persons motivated by challenge . . . . high achievement and accomplishment-oriented people . . . . who are already a part of that denomination. Inside the brochure were lists of activities. The reader was urged to come and fulfill his commitment.

The brochure for another new congregation has on the front a line drawing of a church, several people, and of a home. The only words on the front of the brochure are, "Your friend next door." It is an appeal to compassion and to community. Inside the brochure were pictures of people sharing events of compassion and community with one another.

Some of the mainline Protestant denominations are experiencing decline because their focus is principally on the motivation of commitment. It is somewhat like a focus on the "advanced trigonometry" of church membership—when in fact many, many people seek out congregations that focus on the "basic math" of compassion, community, and hope.

Do a thoughtful analysis of the predominant motivations present in your congregation. It is not as simple as pounding on commitment. In many areas, dominated by high-tech industry, many key leaders have the two primary motivations of challenge and reasonability—they are scientists and engineers, with an entrepreneurial spirit.

The grassroots of some congregations match with challenge and reasonability. These congregations have a strong track record of action, implementation, and momentum because of this excellent match. This can occur in a community where the two primary motivations are prevalent in both the community and the congregation. Indeed, large numbers of people in these communities share the same two major motivational resources—namely, challenge and reasonability. It is an excellent match across the board.

I find this analysis of motivational resources most intriguing and most helpful. I have developed this material out of my own research and reflections. At the same time, on each occasion I share this with groups and give them the chance to compare the motivational resources among key leaders, grassroots, pastor, and the unchurched, it becomes increasingly self-apparent to them why some congregations have a strong track record of action, implementation, and momentum, and some do not.

In your congregation you can encourage forward a motivational match among key leaders, grassroots, pastor, and unchurched. The more bridging of a motivation gap, the more likely the momentum is to grow. The closer the match, the stronger the track record of action, implementation, and momentum. A motivational match stirs momentum.

2

LEADERS AND KEY OBJECTIVES

ESTABLISHING AN EXCELLENT MATCH

Momentum grows as persons achieve key objectives.

We encourage an effective relationship of persons and key objectives by:

Establishing an excellent match
Developing excellent achievement descriptions
Creating constructive key objectives

When we establish a match with persons and key objectives, we create a strong track record of action, implementation, and momentum. We encourage excellent matches. If there is any mistake congregations make, it is that they tend to match people who are willing—but who will not do the job well—with specific key objectives. The art is to match the competencies of people with key objectives. They will do the job well. They are not simply willing.

When you select your key objectives, choose objectives that you have persons who can do them. We match the plays with the players. We do not match the players to the plays. When we do not have persons who can achieve the objective, we do not do the objective. In encouraging persons to achieve objectives, choose

15

persons who can do them well, not those who are willing. Being willing is distinct from being able to do something well.

Once, as a coach of a baseball team, I had occasion to apply these principles. All season long one of my players had jumped up and down during practice, saying, "Let me pitch, coach, let me pitch!" You get tired of the clamor. In a particular game, I decided to give him a chance to pitch.

One of the hardest things I have had to do as a coach was to walk out to the mound in the first inning. We were nine runs behind. There were no outs. The bases were loaded. I said to the pitcher, "Good friend, this is my fault. This is my mistake. I should have been out here five runs ago. You are our best shortstop. Please, now, go and play shortstop. Sam is coming in as pitcher. With your fielding, the rest of the team's fielding, and Sam's pitching, we will get out of this inning and beyond this game." We did.

Some people are willing to do pastoral and lay visitation but do not do it well, even if they go out to visit week after week. You cannot assume that if they had a bit more commitment and worked harder, somehow their visitation would get better. They will do more harm than good to their own spiritual growth pilgrimage and to the spiritual growth of the persons they visit. Choose persons who are competent to do the visitation well.

The art is to match people with objectives so that the objectives can be reached. The Biblical narrative is quite clear on the diversity of human gifts. People have various strengths, gifts, and competencies and can accomplish certain tasks with an extraordinary degree of achievement. When we match a person with some other task that he or she does not do well, we deny his or her real gifts.

The art is to help people to discover the gifts, strengths, and competencies with which God has blessed their lives. Match their competencies with objectives so that people can share their gifts and competencies in ways that count. They will have a high level of satisfaction in seeing their objective come to fruition.

Congregations with a strong track record of action, implementation, and momentum do *not* focus on getting people to fill slots where the church needs a body. Instead, these congregations focus on helping people to discover where their specific gifts and competencies can best be shared. They do not focus on where the congregation needs help. They focus on where each person can help. They see people as unique resources rather than as a means to fill the congregation's momentary needs. They help each person to match his or her competencies with the most appropriate key objectives.

DEVELOPING EXCELLENT ACHIEVEMENT DESCRIPTIONS

We develop excellent achievement descriptions. Thus, we encourage an effective relationship of persons and key objectives. Momentum moves forward.

We used to develop job descriptions. The focus was on describing a "post," a "job." Those efforts focused on the duties, activities, and responsibilities related to a post. They focused on the "turf" one presided over. They focused on tasks to be done. They created a mentality of activities.

Now, we develop an achievement description. We describe the key objectives the person will have fun achieving. We describe the actions on which the person will focus to achieve the key objectives. The key objectives shape the "job description." It is not that an existing "job description" shapes the key objectives.

More fully put, we focus on the person's gifts, strengths, and competencies and on the person's key objectives. This combination shapes the description of the actions and achievements toward which the person heads. We establish an excellent match between persons and key objectives. Then, together with each person, we develop an excellent achievement description.

This is not a description of what each person will *do*. It is a description of what each person plans to *achieve*. Excellent "achievement descriptions" help persons to successfully achieve their key objectives. Such a job description includes the following components:

Two to four key objectives to be achieved
The few major responsibilities

A generous range of authority
A simple line of accountability
One to two competencies to be developed
Steps for mutual evaluation and improvement

Two to Four Key Objectives

These key objectives state what the person looks forward to achieving. Both the person and the team mutually spell out these objectives. These key objectives connect well with the specific keys your congregation is expanding and adding. Each person can consider this question: "What are the two to four key objectives I look forward to achieving to strengthen our congregation's health and mission?"

A Few Major Responsibilities

Many congregations make the mistake of handing persons a long list of "activities and doings." That immediately places persons on a merry-go-round of busyness. An achievement description lists the few major responsibilities important for a person to fulfill to achieve the objectives he or she plans to accomplish. A few major responsibilities are inherent in achieving specific key objectives.

Too many persons have not had the chance to think through what their major responsibilities are. They are handed a long list of activities and meetings, busyness and doings. They are given a long list of responsibilities. They are encouraged to "get busy."

The focus is on "doings."

Where we begin shapes where we end. When we begin with an achievement description, we end with achievements. When we begin with a job description, we end with a merry-go-round of doings and activities.

The Range of Authority

Give persons generous authority. Do not give a collection of doings and responsibilities, with no or little authority. Never give responsibility without giving authority. Three areas of authority are important to share:

Leadership. Identify and list the persons, teams, groups, task forces, and committees who are directly and appropriately accountable to this person. They look to this person as leader for the objectives they are achieving. What shapes "who looks to who" is the key objective, not posts or positions. The key objective shapes the range of authority.

Decision making. State the range of decisions this person has the authority to make. Give generous decision-making authority. Encourage the person to share their authority wisely and generously.

Financial resources. Detail the range of financial resources this person has available. We do not "starve" key objectives. They are worth achieving. They advance the keys we are expanding and adding. We encourage their accomplishment with the finances that will help.

Accountability

Each person develops a simple line of accountability. The person appreciates and understands to whom he or she is accountable. Simple, straight-line accountability is far better than multiple-line accountability.

Specific Competencies to Be Developed

Help each person identify one or two competencies he or she plans to grow forward. This is an often-overlooked component of a good achievement description. Help each person be in a proactive, growing, building, and developing stance.

Mutual Evaluation and Improvement

Include a process for evaluation. It can include four steps.

1. *Self-evaluation.* The proactive person initiates a self-evaluation of his or her achievements and shortcomings during the previous year. In many congregations, the process has been other-initiated rather than self-initiated.

One adjudicatory developed a big, thick black, notebook for pastoral evaluation, inviting each pastoral committee to evaluate the pastor in each of seventeen distinct categories of ministry. At no point in the whole laborious process was the pastor invited to evaluate his or her own work performance.

This "other-initiated" evaluation process creates, among pastors, passive-aggressive behavior, low-grade hostility, subliminal resentment, and eruptive forms of anger. It creates low morale, despair, depression, and despondency. The grievous problem was that this adjudicatory evaluation process did not invite the pastor to achieve a solid, helpful self-evaluation.

The best way to grow forward proactive, growing pastors is to invite them to initiate the first step in the evaluation process. This is equally important as a foundational principle for all persons in a local congregation.

The "pro" in any field has an on-board self-evaluation process. People grow their competency for self-evaluation by practicing it. In the AA and Al-Anon movements, self-evaluation is central. My spirit is, "If someone wrestling with a difficult addiction can learn how to self-evaluate, we can too."

2. *Coaching.* The coaching step is the one in which a leader shares his or her self-evaluation with a coaching team. The coaching team then shares its helpful wisdom, insights, and suggestions in a mutual, constructive discussion with the person.

3. *Mutual agreement.* The person and the coaching team develop a mutual agreement as to the central strengths and weaknesses of what has been accomplished during the past year.

4. *The coming year.* The person and coaching team look at the coming year of the long-range plan. The person self-initiates his or her sense of the two to four key objectives he or she looks forward to achieving in the coming year. The person suggests the one or two specific competencies he or she plans

to grow forward in the coming year. Then, the coaching team shares its wisdom and suggestions.

In any field, the "pros" are the persons who can look ahead and design the objectives they plan to achieve. They can self-initiate their future achievements that will advance the keys the congregation is expanding and adding.

Strong, healthy congregations have clear achievement descriptions that are mutually developed. This includes a self-initiated evaluation process that helps persons to grow themselves forward. Only you can grow you. No one can grow you for you. God gives you the freedom to grow yourself. God gives you mentors and coaches who will help you grow you.

Persons learn to be leaders. It is not possible to teach someone to become a leader. Leaders learn to be leaders in an environment that fosters key objectives, a few major responsibilities, generous authority, and self-initiated growth and development. We cannot teach someone to be a leader. People *can learn* to be leaders.

Strong, healthy congregations have a strong, healthy momentum. They develop excellent matches between leaders and key objectives.

KEY OBJECTIVES

We create constructive key objectives. We act swiftly. Momentum moves forward.

We are expanding and adding specific central characteristics among the *Twelve Keys.*

These are the key strengths that will advance our congregation. Key strengths invite key objectives. Yes, we will do lots of things in the course of a year. We will be drawn into our share of 80 percenters that achieve 20 percent of the results. Not every objective is a key objective.

An objective is a key objective when it directly advances a strength we are expanding or adding. You do not need to do what I next suggest for all objectives. There are many minor objectives in our lives. For the few key objectives, these guidelines help:

1. ***Write down your key objectives.*** There are two values to written key objectives: distance and passion. First, when a key objective is written down on paper or typed into your computer, you can gain sufficient distance from it so that you can creatively evaluate whether or not this objective is worth achieving.

Many people make a shopping list when they go to the store. They modify and improve the list. They delete and add items to the list. They do this well when they have written down the list. The same is true of key objectives. We have learned how to write our "shopping objectives" in something as simple as shopping. We do the same in advancing key objectives that help persons discover the grace of God.

Second, passion. People achieve objectives for which they have passion. When you write down your key objectives, you are confirming the passion you have to achieve them. When you act on these written key objectives, you are living out your passion to accomplish them.

You have made a covenant of passion . . . . and compassion to achieve them. You have, as it were, "signed on the dotted line." You are confirming with yourself that you plan to achieve them.

2. ***Grow a sense of ownership.*** People achieve key objectives for which they have strong sense of "ownership." It needs to be *their* objective, not something thrust on them by an outsider. The value of including as many people as possible in your long-range planning sessions is this: the more people who are included, the more people who have ownership. It is their long-range plan.

3. ***Make sure your objectives are specific and measurable.*** An excellent key objective is sufficiently specific and measurable that one will know when that objective has been accomplished.

For example, "Add fifteen new parking spaces on the west side of the congregation so we will have a total of seventy-five spaces there by October 1." For example, "Serve two hundred children in Vacation Bible School this summer."

State the objective in such a way that whenever members of the congregation evaluate progress, they can check it off as one they have accomplished. What few key objectives would you like to be celebrating one year . . . . or two years from today? State them specifically and measurably.

Any objective that includes the word *more* is not an objective. Sometimes, congregations develop statements such as "We need more members," "We need more people in the choir," or "We need more youth." The word *more* is a setup for failure. *More* is always one more over the horizon. You can never accomplish *more. More* is a never-ending horizon of failure. The same is true of *better.* How do you know if you have succeeded, if you still need more or better?

4. *Set realistic time horizons.* An excellent key objective includes intermediary time horizons that build toward the desired end result. For example, a congregation might have a key objective to increase the choir from twenty to thirty persons in eighteen months. It would be more helpful to have realistic intermediary objectives, such as increasing the choir from:

Twenty to twenty-three persons by September
Twenty-three to twenty-five persons by Christmas
Twenty-five to twenty-eight persons by Easter
Twenty-eight to thirty persons by September

Steady, progressive growth is more likely to be achieved with these realistic time horizons than with a general objective to grow from twenty to thirty in eighteen months.

5. *Make your objectives realistic and achievable.* An excellent objective stirs our creativity and stretches us just enough that we grow forward and develop our strengths. But, an objective is not some grandiose, glittering generality.

The mistake many congregations make is that they set unrealistic and unachievable objectives. Some people have learned a life orientation and a theological perspective with a built-in compulsiveness toward perfectionism. They set too many goals, too high, to be accomplished too soon. People postpone action to postpone failure.

Compulsive, perfectionistic persons tend to set objectives that are too high and will never realistically be achieved. And since the others in the group innately sense that the objective has set them up to fail, they postpone action because they are seeking to postpone failure. Whenever you see that a group or a person is not mobilizing to accomplish an objective, one of the first things to look at is whether that objective is realistic and achievable.

We send in the plays the players can run.

6. *Develop key objectives that are complementary.* Whenever you construct two or four key objectives to expand a current strength, be sure that they complement, supplement, and mutually reinforce one another. If they are divergent, if they head in different directions, look for a stronger match of objectives.

Congregations are strong and healthy because they are heading in the same direction.

FOUR MISTAKES

Strong, healthy congregations avoid four mistakes. Each of these mistakes slows down momentum. Some congregations have a poor track record of action, implementation, and momentum precisely because they are naive and idealistic about leadership competencies. Some congregations commit four grievous mistakes.

1. The mistake: divide people into two categories, leaders and followers.

Regrettably a few pastors and key leaders have said to me that they categorize people into two classes, winners and losers. Fortunately, few people hold that jaundiced view.

I reject even the milder position that some people are leaders and some are followers. At certain times, each of us serves as a leader and, at other times, each serves as a follower. The roles interchange based on the objective, the occasion, the group of people involved, and the specific competencies called for at that time.

Virtually every person has served both as leader and as follower. These are dynamic, developmental roles and people cannot be classified permanently in either one. Strong, healthy congregations live with the confidence that persons can share in each role, based on the objective toward which we are heading.

2. The mistake: miss the fact that there is a diversity of gifts, strengths, and competencies.

Some congregations make the mistake of assuming all persons have the same range of competencies. In their recruiting, they assume anybody can do any job. Indeed, they recruit the job rather than the person.

In fact, people have a vast range of distinctive competencies. We can understand this in two ways. First, one way to understand this is with distinctive ways of learning. Persons learn all of the following ways. You can grow forward any of these distinctive learning ways. And, in a given stage of life, people have a propensity to learn more fully in one or two of these ways:

Physical, athletic
Cognitive, intellectual
Work project, extracurricular
Social, relational
Music and arts
Fad of the moment
Outcast
Independent

For a specific key objective, intellectual, cognitive may be the gift that helps. For another, specific key objective, social, relational may be the competency that helps.

Second, we can understand that persons bring varying strengths, to a greater or lesser degree, to a key objective.

Compassion and caring
Wisdom and discernment
Shepherding and serving
Motivating and leading
Data and analysis
Relational and social

All six are present in every person. And, at the same time, one of the six is likely to be the most developed, predominant competency within an individual at a given point in his or her life's pilgrimage. In a particular setting, with a specific objective and grouping, his or her distinctive competency will be decisive. In those conditions that individual will serve as leader.

When data and analysis competencies are important, the person who has developed that competency will serve as leader. When relational and social competencies are important, the person who has developed that competency will serve as leader. Furthermore, the diversity of gifts is broader than even these six strengths. People cannot be classified simply as leaders or followers. The assumption that leaders have essentially the same leadership competencies is foolish.

Strong, healthy congregations confirm that there is a diversity of gifts. For each individual, each of his or her strengths will be helpful with a distinctive key objective.

Healthy congregations do not assume some people are leaders and some are followers. They do not assume leaders have essentially the same leadership competencies.

They do not assume any leader can be plugged into any leadership role—so long as he or she is willing. They do not assume that if someone is given a job, he or she will, therefore, become a leader. They do assume that there is a diversity of gifts. They honor the diversity of gifts that each person brings to the mission

3. The mistake: assume that any current leader can be plugged into any leadership role.

Some congregations tend to commit this mistake as they scramble to fill the empty slots they have in their organizational and committee structures. You can study samples of the leadership surveys and time and talent surveys used in many congregations. Most are primarily designed to find people to fill the congregation's needs. Mostly, these lists contain lengthy descriptions of posts, jobs, and committee positions.

Congregations with a strong record of momentum focus on helping persons discover their specific gifts, strengths, and competencies. The spirit is to help the persons discover the specific key objective their gifts can best help the congregation to achieve. The focus is not where they can fill some slot.

4. The mistake: assume that, if you give someone a job, he or she will become a leader.

Some congregations are particularly prone to do this with new members. They assume that giving the new member a job will help him or her to become a leader. When the new member is given the wrong job, we are on our way to creating a new inactive member. A poor match is made. It does not work out. The person realizes that his or her distinctive gifts were not taken seriously. The person becomes quietly gun shy. He or she drifts into the woodwork.

The mistake is to give a person a key objective that does not match with his or her strengths. The person may function with a leadership value of 1 to 4 because of the poor match. When the person is given a key objective that is an excellent match, the person's leadership contribution will be an 8, 9, or 10. You can practice having a realistic assessment of the leadership competencies present with persons.

We establish an excellent match. We develop excellent achievement descriptions. We create constructive key objectives. We do not make four mistakes. We have fun. We live in the grace of God. We stir and advance the momentum of our congregation.

3

AN EFFECTIVE
LONG-RANGE PLAN

Momentum has power with an effective long-range plan.

Momentum begins with motivation. Momentum grows as persons achieve key objectives. We create an effective long-range plan. Momentum builds. An effective long-range plan includes these distinctive qualities:

> Our plan includes only 20 percenters.
> Our plan matches with our current strengths.
> Our plan matches with the community and mission field our congregation seeks to serve.
> Our plan builds on the plays the players can run.
> Our plan does not set too many objectives.

When you confirm that your plan includes these qualities, you have an effective long-range plan. You will build momentum. Your momentum will have power.

ONLY 20 PERCENTERS

An effective long-range plan includes only the 20 percenters that yield 80 percent of the results.

Whenever even one or two 80 percenters creep in, that long-range plan loses its effectiveness. The inclusion of even one or two 80 percenters gives rise to yet a third and then a fourth.

They multiply like dandelions. Once one or two get in, before you know it there are ten or fifteen or fifty, or a hundred.

We could ask ourselves why an 80 percenter creeps into our plan. Sometimes, it is because we have not clearly enough decided the keys among the twelve we are planning to expand and add. Once we are clear on our "expands and adds," we have a sound basis for deciding what is in our plan, and what is not in our plan.

Sometimes, we have not practiced our ability to discern between a 20 percenter and an 80 percenter. This is true in life and well as in church. We all learn what is of value and importance. In good times, we spend money as though it were growing on trees and going out of style. In tough times, our values center. What is genuinely important becomes clearer and dearer.

Sometimes, the 80 percenters creep in simply because we are tidy persons. We are neat and orderly persons. We like things spick and span. We are uncluttered persons. We come across an idea. It sounds pretty reasonable. We do not want to leave the idea "just lying around." We are reluctant to let it go. Almost without thinking, we include it in the plan.

Sometimes, in our enthusiasm, we allow our latent compulsive addictive perfectionism to take over. It seems to show up without our realizing it. It uses our enthusiasm as a cloak to sneak into the room. There is a major distinction between enthusiasm and perfectionism. Feel free to be enthusiastic about your 20 percenters. Share your enthusiasm with balance, not excess. Share your passion with focus, force, energy, and *direction*.

Excess breeds excess. Once you become distracted with an 80 percenter, someone else will. And someone else will. And someone else. And, before we know it, we are off and running on a racetrack of 80 percenters that simply goes around and around, and never gets anywhere.

The art in life is to discover the few 20 percenters that count. The art in a congregation is to do the same. The best long-range plans include only those 20 percenters that will deliver 80 percent of the results. Think through whether or not each key objective being considered for your long-range plan is a 20 percenter.

OUR PLAN MATCHES WITH OUR CURRENT STRENGTHS

A long-range plan is effective when the central characteristics you plan to expand and add match well with your congregation's current strengths.

Some congregations develop long-range plans that seek to shore up their weaknesses rather than build on their strengths. The art of developing an effective long-range plan is to select one or two of your current strengths among the twelve central characteristics that you can expand. We act swiftly. We move forward now.

The expansion of a current strength helps set up the congregation to succeed, not fail. It gives the congregation a highly visible, quick win. It helps the congregation to develop a sense of momentum. Working on a weakest weakness takes a long, long time. There is no quick win. Congregations lose heart. They become further discouraged. They settle back into despair, discouragement, and despondency.

When a congregation takes a current strength, an 8 on a scale of 1 to 10, and grows forward the strength to a 9 or a 10, momentum moves. It is more fun to score in the first quarter. Congregations benefit from a 20 percenter that is a highly visible quick win.

The next step is to select one central characteristic you want to build forward into a new strength. Note that we expand a current strength before we add a new strength. We practice success by expanding a current strength. We do better what we do best.

By expanding a current strength, we build our confidence. We build our assurance. We build our momentum. We are in the strongest place to add a new strength. The art is to add a new strength that matches well with the strengths already well in place. The long-range planning process that achieves this will build momentum for your congregation.

OUR PLAN MATCHES WITH THE COMMUNITY AND MISSION FIELD OUR CONGREGATION SEEKS TO SERVE

A congregation develops momentum as its plan matches with the community and mission field the congregation seeks to serve. As your congregation thinks about expanding and adding key strengths, look for a fitting match with the community and with the mission field your congregation seeks to serve.

After seeing the large number of gray-haired persons in the congregation, a church, in Florida, decided the future of the congregation was at stake. So they invested $1.3 million in building a gymnasium to attract youth so that the church would survive after the older people were gone. The gym sits empty most of the time.

This congregation could have matched its long-range plan with the community and mission field God gives it to serve. The leaders would have realized that the future of the congregation is not endangered. The new "youth" who will see to the ongoing future of that congregation in the coming twenty-five years are retiring from Indiana, Ohio, Pennsylvania, and New York to that part of Florida.

They are moving to the south and settling in that part of Florida. They will continue to do so over the coming quarter of a century. The congregation would have been better off developing one major mission outreach, shepherding visitation, and one competent program focused on recently retired people, rather than on youth. This would constitute a better match with the community and mission field available to that congregation.

I help many congregations where there is no one in the church under sixty-five years of age. This is because there is no one in the community under sixty-five years of age. For many congregations in Florida, Arizona, and New Mexico, the "children's division" are persons sixty to seventy-five years of age. The "youth division" is for persons seventy-five to eighty-five. The "adult division" is for persons eighty-five and above.

It is not true that a congregation, to be strong and healthy, has to have persons from the cradle to the grave. It is true that the congregation benefits from a plan and sense of direction that matches with the persons God gives us to serve. With this match, we will have momentum.

OUR PLAN BUILDS ON THE PLAYS THE PLAYERS CAN RUN

We increase momentum when we send in the plays the players can run. The key objectives are ones the congregation can accomplish. Some congregations, regretfully, try to fit their expands, adds, and key objectives into an already existing organizational structure of their denomination.

The art is to never send in plays the players cannot run. The art is to never send in more plays than the players can run. The art is to create a structure that grows out of our expands, adds, and key objectives. An effective long-range plan has a reasonable number of objectives that match best with the players, the leadership team, and the strengths, gifts, and competencies with which God has blessed them.

Function shapes form. Strategy shapes structure. Objectives shape organization. We do not do it the other way around. The helpful, effective order is:

1. Decide your strengths to expand and add.
2. Select your key objectives that will achieve your expand and add.
3. Discover the persons who will achieve these objectives.
   Actually, we do these first three almost together.
4. Shape your organizational structure to match with what you plan to achieve.

Too many congregations reverse the order. They begin with an existing organizational structure. Then, they try to fit their new future into an old organization structure. It does not work with new wine. It does not work to grow a strong, healthy congregation.

I suggest to congregations, especially those that are weak and declining or dying, "The old structure, if it were going to have worked, it would worked by now. Maybe, in the long lost past, it did work. In recent times, you have redoubled and tripled your efforts to make it work. Maybe, now is the time to let it go."

As one grouping knows well, "Insanity is redoubling our efforts on something that is not working, expecting new and better results."

In our time, people give generous efforts to grow forward strengths and objectives they see will make a difference. They have no "passion" to preserve an old organizational structure. They do have "passion" for strengths and key objectives they have helped to decide and for which they have ownership.

Thus, create just enough people on just enough achievements teams that we achieve our objectives. These teams stir their compassion. They achieve wise decisions. Significant results are accomplished. We shape the structure to help, not hinder, the teams. Momentum grows. The lives of many people are blessed with the grace of God.

OUR PLAN DOES NOT SET TOO MANY OBJECTIVES

We increase momentum when we do not set too many objectives.

The Callahan Principle is "Plan less to achieve more." Do not focus on more central characteristics than can reasonably be accomplished within your specified time horizon. The art is to focus on the few decisive central characteristics and the related key objectives that will best expand and add those characteristics.

Some congregations assume that the more key objectives, the better the plan. Some congregations assume that the more pages to their planning document, the better the plan. As a matter of fact, the more pages included, the fewer the people who will help to achieve the plan.

Planning expands to fill the time available. Plans tend to expand to fill the number of sheets of paper available. Limit the time. Limit the number of sheets of paper. Limit the number of gigabytes in your computer. Limit the number of key objectives. Then, your congregation can focus on the 20 percenters that match your current strengths, the community and mission field you serve, and the leadership team available. Have the spirit that you plan to select a few key objectives and achieve them. That creates the dynamic of spillover impact on the work and mission of your congregation.

Too many objectives demotivate people. A long list of chores is demotivation. Some persons think that if they demotivate people that people will do better. Under threat, people wither. With encouragement, people grow. The threat, "If you do not quit drinking, you are going to die" is demotivating. The alcoholic is reminded that life is short. There is much to drink. He wants to do his part. He drinks more.

The statement, "If you do not do all of these objectives, your church is going to die," creates a congregation that becomes tense, tight, nervous, and anxious. They are good people. They want to do their part. They manufacture a busy collection of objections.

They work harder. They die gently.

No one is drawn to a tense, tight, nervous, and anxious group of people. They are not drawn to a grouping that is busy and bustling, trying to do too much. People are drawn to a grouping that is having fun, with a relaxed spirit, and an intentional sense of direction to achieve a few key objectives.

I learned a long time ago in coaching basketball that the art is to help each player discover his or her best shot. When the players practice shooting, they focus on their best shot, so that seven out of ten times, as the ball leaves their hands, they have the confidence, assurance, and competence that the ball is going in the basket.

This increases the probability that, when they get the ball in another part of the court, their confidence, assurance, and competence will "spill over." They will be more likely to make the shot. Some players practice shots all over the court. They never discover and focus on their best shot. They end up with mediocre shooting records. Those who focus on their best shot grow forward an excellent team and a strong track record of action, implementation, and momentum.

Momentum grows as a congregation develops an effective long-range plan:

Including only 20 percenters

Matching with our current strengths

Matching with the community and mission field our congregation seeks to serve

Building on the plays the players can run

Having not too many objectives

God encourages you to move forward. God blesses you with momentum. God blesses you with grace.

4

EXCELLENT MISTAKES AND OBJECTIVES WORTH NOT DOING

EXCELLENT MISTAKES

Momentum moves forward as we discover the value of excellent mistakes.

Momentum begins with a motivational match. Momentum grows as persons achieve key objectives. Momentum develops power with an effective long-range plan. Momentum moves forward as we discover, honor, and cherish the value of excellent mistakes.

Congregations who value and honor excellent mistakes have momentum. These congregations have developed a community value for appreciating, recognizing, and rewarding lessons learned from excellent mistakes.

There is a direct correlation between excellent mistakes and the level of creativity and productivity in any congregation. The more a congregation appreciates, recognizes, and rewards excellent mistakes, the higher the level of creativity and productivity in the organization. The organization that is not making mistakes is the organization that is not doing anything.

Some years ago when we first took up sailing, I was concerned about the possibility that we might run aground—that the sailboat's deep keel would lodge on a sandbar or reef. As we talked with other sailors, it soon became clear that the old saying was true:

> The skipper who says he has never run aground, his boat
> has never left the dock.

We are bound to run aground sometime. We are also likely to make excellent mistakes. Some congregations become anxious and fearful about making mistakes. They never "leave the dock." Their boat never sets sail.

Focus on moving ahead, rather than focusing on avoiding mistakes. Encourage and build the understanding that some mistakes will happen. We don't want them to happen. We will do our level best to help them to not happen. But, if we make a mistake, we will learn from it, and we will seek to not make the same mistake again.

The baseball player knows he or she will not get a hit each time at bat, but he or she still goes to bat. Often, a player flies out or strikes out. Sometimes, he or she is thrown out at first. It doesn't work to expect a home run each time at bat. However, very few baseball players get anywhere by staying in the dugout or by never stepping up to the plate. We need to do as these players do—go to the plate with a relaxed intentionality to do well on this pitch and to learn from any excellent mistakes we make.

Valuing lessons learned from excellent mistakes cannot be construed as an *excuse* for condoning mistakes. Some congregations adopt a *"poor little me"* attitude, thinking they can never do anything right. They expect that their chances of doing anything right are slim. Sure enough, it becomes a self-fulfilling prophecy. They never do anything right. They do not even achieve mediocrity.

Healthy congregations value excellent, solid, creative, risk-taking mistakes. These mistakes are sometimes costly. And, in creative, constructive ways, we learn substantially and beneficially from these mistakes.

For years, I have been convinced of my principle: people lead the way they experience being led. Recently, I was teaching at the seminary of a denomination in which there is a theological perspective that encourages a kind of compulsiveness toward perfectionism. In many respects, the ministers of that denomination are encouraged *never* to make a mistake. Indeed, it is the practice that mistakes they make are noted on their personnel record, which follows them for most of their ministerial life.

I was meeting with the faculty of that seminary at their annual retreat, serving as their resource leader and consultant. We were discussing this specific dilemma. Various members of the faculty reflected on the consequences of this pattern. They asked my wisdom on the matter.

I suggested that the pattern creates ministers who are tense, tight, nervous, anxious, fearful, cautious, and nonrisking—who do what is minimally expected of them in passive, reactive ways. There is not a great deal of creativity. There is not a great deal of action. There is not a great deal of achievement and accomplishment. There was a general nodding of heads in agreement. Various faculty shared comments confirming and adding to these suggestions.

People lead in direct relation to the way they experience being led. At the retreat, we talked about my further thought: people teach in direct relation to the way they experience being taught. People minister in direct relation to the way in which they experience being ministered to.

I suggested to the faculty that they could have an excellent year of teaching and helping their students. In the spring, they could have the fun of discussing together and thinking through who among the faculty had learned the most from making "an excellent mistake" during the year. I suggested that part of the honors program in the spring could be the presentation to the faculty member who had successfully made the "excellent mistake" of the year.

This would not be a "hazing" or a "making fun of" the person or the excellent mistake. It would be a serious honoring and valuing of what we have learned from the excellent mistake. I suggested that one of the important learnings they could share with their students is the ability to learn from excellent mistakes.

This would confirm with the students that excellent mistakes are appreciated, valued, and honored. When professors are never wrong, it teaches students to never be wrong. When professors honor and value excellent mistakes, it gives students permission to, from time to time, make and learn from an excellent mistake.

I have been in congregations where someone twenty-five years before said that that congregation was doomed. Twenty-five years have come and gone. Yes, there are fewer people. They all have graying hair. But the congregation has hung on and clung to a bare, meager existence for over a quarter of a century. The problem began, way back then, with the fear of doing anything out of the fear of failure. In weak and declining and dying congregations there is a sense in which people freeze, become immobilized, and are afraid to do anything for fear they might do something wrong.

One of the healthiest gifts we can share is the understanding that congregations are tough, resilient, long-lasting creations of God. They last a long, long time. The art is to creatively and constructively move forward. We understand that some of the key objectives we include in our long-range plan may turn out to be excellent mistakes. This is one of the reasons we advance our plan, we replan, each year.

Some people wisely suggest, "The first plan is always wrong. We plan. Then, we replan." This is said as an act of grace. The thought that the first plan is always wrong confirms three important principles:

1. Even with the best of intentions to not do so, we may include an excellent mistake in our first plan.
2. Relax. The best plans can be improved. We can do so. We act swiftly. We improve our plan swiftly.
3. We learn as we go. What looked like an excellent idea in the beginning is turning out to be an excellent mistake. What counts is what we learn from our mistake. We are not counting the number of mistakes. We are counting what we learn from them.

In their classic work, ***In Search of Excellence,*** Tom Peters and Bob Waterman have identified a bias for action as a common thread among America's best-run companies. Our congregation benefits from a bias for action. Indeed, if the choice has to be made, a congregation is better off to choose slightly unco-ordinated action over fully coordinated inaction. The premium placed on coordination in many of the major denominations is precisely one of the reasons those denominations are in trouble. It is as though they must coordinate everything neatly and tidily so as to ensure that everyone is together and no mistake will ever be made.

We need more creativity and less coordination. We need more action, accomplishment, and achievement and fewer meet-ings and less coordination. The desire to never make a mistake is the decision to demotivate everyone in the congregation. If you want to fear something, fear demotivation. Demotivation will do real damage and harm in your congregation. With demotivation, people roll over and play dead.

Strong, healthy congregations discover, honor, and cherish the value of an excellent mistake. They learn from it. They encour-age creativity, innovation, initiative, and productivity. They encourage people to act swiftly. Momentum moves forward.

OBJECTIVES WORTH NOT DOING

Momentum moves forward as we recognize some objectives are worth not doing.

Many congregations act swiftly. They have a strong track record for action, implementation, and momentum. They know some objectives are worth not doing. In even the most effective long-range plans, there may be two or three key objectives that turn out to be excellent mistakes. It is equally true, even in the best long-range plans, that there may be one or two key objec-tives that are worth not doing.

Sometimes, we do not work on some key objectives because we sense the failure implicit in them. Most persons and most groups gravitate toward success, not failure.

Sometimes, when we closely analyze why a congregation has not accomplished some of its key objectives, we discover that those key objectives may very well have set up that congregation to fail, not succeed. Some key objectives may appear to be excellent in the early stages of developing an effective long-range plan. But as the congregation puts the plan into place and the dynamic of momentum begins to move forward, it becomes clear that one or two key objectives are worth not doing.

There is a difference between valuing excellent mistakes and recognizing that an objective is worth not doing. In a congregation that values excellent mistakes, some person, task force, or committee tries to accomplish a key objective and in the process achieves an excellent mistake. Deciding an objective is worth not doing is a decision we make before someone has started to work on that key objective.

In the best long-range plans, one or two key objectives fall by the wayside. No one takes up the banner to lead them forward. Why does that happen? Sometimes, it happens because:

1. No one senses, finally, a good match with that key objective.
2. The motivational resources connected with that objective do not match with the motivations of the grassroots.
3. People sense innately that the objective is of lesser priority than other objectives we plan to achieve.
4. People sense the objective is a setup for failure, not success.

Healthy congregations have the value that some objectives are worth not doing. They are realistic in evaluating the past and improving plans for the coming years, including adding the new year in their plan.

Some congregations discover several objectives they intended to accomplish but have not achieved. They begin to berate themselves for a lack of commitment. They have now become the slaves of their own plan. The plan is dominating their perspective and perception. They redouble their efforts. They add more objectives. They set themselves up to fail. The principle is: the plan is always the creature of those who have created it.

We work the plan. The plan does not work us.

With this value strongly in place as part of our corporate self-understanding, we can let some objectives go, forget them, and understand that in the end they were not worth doing. This decision is reached in light of the objectives we are accomplishing and in the light of those objectives that, for us, have been excellent mistakes and from which we have learned in constructive, creative ways.

Some congregations cling to an objective created four years before simply because it was created four years before and they feel they should do something with it.

Finally, some objectives are worth letting go and not doing.

More Help Than Would Be Helpful. *One practice worth not doing is giving more help than would be helpful.* Momentum moves forward when we share almost enough help to be helpful. Momentum slows down when we give more help than would be helpful. The art is to share just enough help to be helpful, but not so much help that the help is harmful and creates a pattern of dependency and co-dependency. To deliver more help than is helpful is to deliver coddling, not caring. It is to create a dependent person, not a growing, developing person.

Years ago, while working with persons who wrestle with alcoholism, I learned this. When helping persons allow themselves to be controlled by the person they are trying to help, they simply prove they do not have the competencies to help. I have met myself coming and going in situations when someone, who could not control his own behavior, ran me around the mulberry bush . . . . many times. When a person, say an alcoholic, who cannot control his own behavior, learns he can control my behavior, I have just taught the person I am not a source of help.

Intuitively, the alcoholic senses that what he needs is a helping person who can control his own behavior, who can live life with a reasonable amount of balance.

We allow ourselves to be controlled, primarily because we are intent on giving help. We end up delivering more help than would be helpful. In the early days of sharing in a mission with people who wrestle with alcoholism, I ran into my fair share of difficulty. The third time I got myself beat up by an alcoholic, I asked myself, "What am I doing to contribute to my being beat up?"

The three events happened with three different persons I was trying to help. The events happened over a period of time. The three persons did not know one another. I was the only consistent person in all three events. With one event, particularly, I found myself getting my head slammed against a wall, early on a Saturday morning, wondering whether I was going to come out alive.

It dawned on me. The discovery had been sitting in front of me. These days, I share my discovery with what I call the Callahan Principle for Helping:

Balance breeds balance.

Excess breeds excess.

Excess breeds excess. Excessive helpfulness breeds excessive resistance. It does not breed excessive gratefulness. It does not breed excessive gratitude. I was trying to be too helpful. I was trying to do too much. In effect, the three persons were trying to say to me,

Get away from me with all your helpfulness. Deep down, I understand this is my problem, not your problem. I am angry with myself. I am angry with you. With all your helpfulness, you remind me too much of all my failures. Quit giving me so much help.

Balance breeds balance. The mistake many persons make in giving help is that they share more help than is helpful. The art is to share just enough help to be helpful, and no more. The art is to keep the problem with the person. The art is to not take the problem on yourself. When we do that, they, then, can do nothing with their problem. Intuitively, they know it is their problem to solve.

We can share wisdom and experience. We can share encouragement and support. We can help them to be part of a grouping where they discover roots, place, and belonging. We can deliver coaching. We can help them discover one strength, yet remaining, that is a strength they have. This one strength, however feeble and fragile, is the rock on which they can build forward their future. We can let the problem stay with them. We can give just enough help to be helpful, but not too much.

Grassfires. *One practice worth not doing is giving too much attention to grassfires . . . . running frequently to put out grassfires.* Some person starts a "grassfire." People, out of their own anxiety and out of a desire to be helpful, come running to put out the grassfire. They deliver attention, affection, recognition, and dependency.

They teach the person that one of the best things he or she can do next is to start another grassfire. People will come running to help put it out again. They deliver attention, affection, recognition, and dependency. A cycle is created of starting grassfires and people who come running to put them out. Indeed, the cycle may have been there long before we showed up to help.

I distinguish between a grassfire and a forest fire. When it is a grassfire, give the person the chance to learn from his or her mistake rather than protecting him or her from failure. I say this next, gently. One of the best friends, one of the best teachers an alcoholic has is pain.

When the pain is quickly relieved, when we take away the pain, the person loses a good friend and a good teacher. When someone comes running to put out a grassfire, the helping person removes one of the most constructive friends and teachers the alcoholic has available—namely, the pain associated with learning from a good friend and a good teacher.

One time, a child set off fireworks in a vacant lot and started a real grassfire. People nearby pitched in to put it out. Even the fire department was called to help put it out. Once the damage had been contained, the child's aunt had a discussion with the child to be sure she understood what she had done, how much fright it had caused the neighbors (fortunately, in this case, no serious property damage occurred), what might have happened, and what behavior was expected, indeed, counted on—in the future.

It was a calm, gentle, firm conversation. There was no excessive nervousness or panic. There was no yelling or shouting. There was no beating or punishment. There was no pushing and shoving. There was no recrimination. The conversation had a spirit of balance. The child never started another grassfire.

When a "grassfire" happens in a congregation, people rush to help, wanting to minimize the damage. All too often, the person responsible gets an overdose of supportive concern and forgiveness or an overdose of yelling and shouting or, worse yet, both. They get an "underdose" of coaching and accountability. What helps is a coaching conversation, calm and firm, with the person who started the "fire." The spirit is one of balance.

Excess creates passive, dependent persons who learn to start new grassfires because people come running to deliver attention, affection, recognition, and dependency. Sometimes, someone says to me, "If we don't come running and put out the grassfire, it will turn into a forest fire."

I suggest, "Give persons a chance to put out the grassfire they started. They will learn. If you put it out for them, they will never learn. I take that back. Yes, they will. They will learn that when they start the next grassfire, we will come running." To be sure, we will help with a forest fire. We will not assume every grassfire is going to turn into a forest fire. Frequently, the person puts it out.

A forest fire looks like a situation where major bodily, emotional, and spiritual damage is harming many people. Lives are at stake. The escalation is soaring, moving well out of control. We help. We help with a calm, confident spirit. We have a presence of grace. We have a sense of reassurance. We do not share excessive behavior. We share balance.

Let me reiterate this point. I am *not* suggesting that persons be ignored. In all of my coaching, I have followed the practice, the policy that whoever shows up for practice plays. Mostly, we go with the team we have. We coach them forward. The danger of investing coaching time in putting out every grassfire is that one creates a pattern of dependency and passivity.

Two major demotivators with people are: (1) giving more help than would be helpful, and (2) focusing too much on grassfires.

As a wise, helpful coach, I count on my left fielder to catch the fly ball. I cannot run out and catch it for him. I count on the person at bat to bunt down the first base line and beat the throw. I cannot bat for him. I count on my catcher to call solid signals for the pitcher. I cannot call signals for him. What I can do is deliver just enough coaching and encouragement that the team has the confidence, assurance, and competencies that they will play well. We will win the game together. We will help one another. We will not *over help*.

Strong, healthy congregations act swiftly. They grow forward both the value of excellent mistakes and the value that some objectives are finally worth not doing. Momentum moves forward.

5

MEMORY, CHANGE, CONFLICT, AND HOPE

THE DYNAMIC OF MEMORY

Momentum deepens as we value memory, change, conflict, and hope.

These four dynamics contribute enormously to the momentum of a congregation.

Memory
Change
Conflict
Hope

These four dynamics are present in every person and in every grouping of people. They are present in your own life's pilgrimage. These four dynamics have a distinctive configuration in each congregation. They have major impact on any present moment and, indeed, on any future moment in the life of your congregation. Understanding these four dynamics will be helpful to you as you deepen your own life . . . . as you deepen the momentum in your congregation.

From one congregation to another, memory, change, conflict, and hope live themselves out in distinctive ways. I encourage you to have a spirit of compassion and a depth of wisdom as to the unique, distinctive ways these dynamics are influencing the present understandings, perceptions, and behaviors in your local

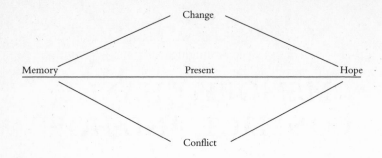

congregation. You can assist your congregation in being aware of the ways in which distinctive events of memory, change, conflict, and hope have contributed and continue to contribute to the shaping of the perceptions and behaviors present in your congregation . . . . and of the momentum in your congregation.

Memory is strong because memory is about the past events that decisively contribute to our present understandings and perceptions, and our anticipations and hopes for the future. We remember five kinds of events that contribute to our perceptions and our behavior:

Tragic events. We remember tragic events that mar and scar our lives. These memories profoundly affect our sense of the present and future as well as the past.

Sinful events. We remember sinful events in which we have participated. We ask God's forgiveness and the forgiveness of others for our participation in those sinful events.

Incidental events. We remember incidental events. We do not know quite why we remember them, but they are present with us and shape our current perceptions and future anticipations.

Celebrative events. We remember celebrative events, birthdays, baptisms, graduations, anniversaries, events in which we celebrate accomplishments and achievements. We remember events of good fun and good times, family reunions.

Hope-fulfilling events. Most important, we remember hope-fulfilling events. We remember those events in which our deepest longings, yearnings, and hopes were decisively fulfilled.

Some people make the mistake of assuming that congregations are primarily creatures of custom, habit, and tradition. To be sure, congregations develop richly and fully a wide range of distinctive customs, habits, and traditions.

When one looks closely at the traditions present in a congregation, one discovers that the most powerful traditions are not about events of memory in an historical, chronological sense of the past. The most powerful, profound traditions congregations celebrate recall those events in which the congregation's own hopes for the future were most dramatically and decisively fulfilled.

One congregation had some of its deepest longings, yearnings, and hopes decisively fulfilled in an event in 1886. What they have done in 1887, 1888, 1889, and every year since has been to celebrate and honor, to relive, that event. They have developed the tradition of honoring that longed-for, future-based, hope-fulfilling event.

One reason memory is strong is that memory is about hope. It is in memory that people remember these events of hope. This is what Passover is about. This is what the Exodus is about. This is what the Open Tomb and Risen Lord and New Life in Christ are about. These are not events of the past. These are events in which the future of our hopes has been decisively fulfilled.

With a sense of prayerfulness and with a good-fun, relaxed spirit, consider the dynamic of memory as it distinctively lives itself out in your congregation. Think of the several events of memory decisive for your congregation. With compassion and wisdom, come to understand these events, whether tragic, sinful, incidental, celebrative, or hope-fulfilling. These events inform and enrich, encourage and discourage, motivate and demotivate, influence and shape your present moments and your perceptions of the future. As you come to understand these events, value them, and come to peace about them, you will deepen the momentum of your congregation.

THE DYNAMIC OF CHANGE

Two kinds of change have forceful impact upon a congregation.

External changes
Internal changes

Many congregations are sensitive to external changes that have affected them and will continue to affect them in the future. Such external changes include the establishment of a strong, dynamic new congregation half a mile away, which now vibrantly contributes nine out of the twelve central characteristics of strong, healthy congregations. A significant external change is the building of a six-lane highway that has shaped, in fresh new ways, the traffic direction patterns of a community. A significant external change is the opening or closing of a factory.

External changes abound. They are all around us. They move swiftly. These changes are:

Life stage	Civic and community
Human hurt and hope	Scientific
Economic	Medical
Educational	Music and arts
Societal	Recreational
Political	Environmental
Missional	Demographic
Vocational	Geographical
Religious	

These have strong impact on a local congregation. You can discuss with a gathering some of the distinctive external changes that are affecting your congregation. Consider which of these are major external changes for your congregation.

Most importantly, think through the internal sources of change that decisively contribute to the dynamics of your congregation:

Birth and death
Coming and leaving
Growing and developing

Regrettably, some congregations become preoccupied with the external sources of change. Equally important, and sometimes more important, are the internal sources of change that contribute substantially and significantly to a congregation's strengths, character, and momentum.

Birth and Death. Some people are born and some people die. This is one major internal source of change. Birth can have as profound an impact as death. At First Congregation, the small group of young couples began to start families. The congregation began to think in ways it had not considered for twenty years. Perhaps, God is inviting us to share a mission outreach with young families. They began to think of the possibilities for shepherding. They began to consider the possibilities for worship.

It had been years since anyone had been back in the nursery. They began to think of the possible need for a new nursery, a new young couples' class, and a preschool program. They began to think of encouraging some of their best shepherds and teachers to focus with preschool families. They began including these young couples on leadership teams.

Some people die. At Pleasant Valley Church, which was anything but pleasant some of the time, Lois had been the linking person in a two-cell church. Pleasant Valley was richly and fully a two-cell congregation. The best thing two-cell congregations do, and they do it extraordinarily well, is fight. This was a fight between the old-timers and the newcomers, the pioneers and the homesteaders, the cattlemen and the sheepherders. And the fight was on. Now, the newcomers were not that new. They came thirty years ago, but, from the point of view of the old-timers, they are newcomers.

The seasonal conflicts between the old-timers and the newcomers ranged from:

> "Someone has moved the kitchen utensils from where they have always been."
> "Someone has moved the chair from where it has always been."
> "This is not your parking place."
> "This is not your pew."

to:

> "He has been chair of the committee long enough."
> "We should stay at our old location."
> "We should move to the new location."
> "We like our choir director."
> "We need a new choir director."

In a two-cell congregation, the list goes on and on. There will be a fight. Then, there will be a time of truce, resting up, and gaining energies for the next fight. These conflicts have a seasonal rhythm.

At Pleasant Valley, Lois was the daughter of the patriarch of the old-timers. She was married to one of the newcomers. She provided a constructive, although tenuous, link that minimized the intensity of the fighting.

Late one Saturday evening, coming back from a teachers' meeting in the heavy rains of that fall, a semi-tractor-trailer smashed to smithereens the car in which Lois and five other teachers rode. The link between the two cells was no more. The congregation was now a two-cell congregation with all the richness of anger and fury over the loss of the favorite daughter. The hope for the future was dead. The sense of anger and fury and terror compounded an already tenuous situation. Lois' death was a decisive change.

Or consider this example. Mr. Smith was for years the "glue" that held Piney Grove congregation together. Piney Grove was an open and welcoming, warm and inclusive, large one-cell congregation. Mr. Smith was the glue. When Mr. Smith died, there was no one available to take his place, to do as well as he did the "gluing" of that congregation. The congregation became a splintered, disparate collection of factions that wandered now here, now there, without any sense of cohesiveness. One source of change is that some people are born and some people die.

Coming and Leaving. A second internal source of change is the coming and leaving of people. In a given congregation, the central leader of the music program was transferred by her employer to another community. A year later, people were discussing the fact that their pastor's preaching was not what it used to be.

Upon closer examination it was discovered that before the music leader had been transferred as choir director, she had been delivering a choir of thirty highly motivated, enthusiastic persons each Sunday. The music was dynamic and inspiring. When she was transferred, the church leaders did the best they could to replace her as choir director. The new choir director was an excellent person, young—in her early twenties—and doing the best she could. When I heard the phrase "doing the best she could," I knew what had happened. The total impact of the service was not as dynamic and inspiring as it had been.

The choir was down to seventeen members. Their singing was not as stirring and inspiring. Sometimes, there were only ten in the choir on Sunday. This was down from a choir of thirty who sang with a stirring, inspiring spirit. But the church members felt that surely it could not be the homegrown choir director, "doing the best she could," who was responsible for the loss of a stirring, helpful worship service. It must have to do with the preaching.

The converse is equally the case. I have been in congregations across the land where the coming of new people with rich new gifts and competencies has substantially helped to grow forward a given congregation. To be sure, in some communities one is considered a newcomer until he or she has lived there for eighteen or more years. At the same time, many people, moving into the new community, coming new to a congregation, have excellent skills in getting on board quickly.

Equally important, some of the people who come new are not really newcomers. I remember the Sunday when Bill came first to congregation. He was the chief of the volunteer fire department in the community. He was an excellent person, and he was also known to have his fair share of problems with drinking. That Sunday, as he walked in, there was a hush. Reluctantly at first, and then fully and richly, the congregation accepted Bill. The congregation was never the same from that day forward because of the arrival of that one person.

In another congregation, there were twelve in the choir. In the choir that Sunday morning was a fifteen-year-old girl who was clearly very pregnant under her choir robe.

She had come, pregnant and unmarried. Her family had turned her out. She lived with her aunt for a time. Then, her aunt turned her out.

For a few nights, she had slept in a small shed at the back of the lumberyard. The nights were getting cold. Cooler weather was on the way. She did not know where to turn. No one would have anything to do with her. Word had spread.

On Sunday morning, she found her way to a church. Not her own church, in which she had grown up. In that last fiery, eruptive conversation with her parents, she had been warned to never come to the "family" church. She was cut off.

She was drawn to a church. She stumbled into this church, not knowing anything about it. She had never been there before. She just could not go on anymore. This congregation was more conservative than her childhood church. Their theology was sterner. Their moral standards were higher. They were of "old stock." They lived mostly in a time that had come and gone. They were of the "old school."

They took her in.

No one knows why. They just did.

The congregation was a new congregation from that Sunday on.

Growing and Developing. The third source of internal change is that some people grow and develop. Some people do not. As people grow and develop in their own life's pilgrimage, their contributions, perspective, and perceptions for their own congregation grow and develop as well. To be sure, John was an excellent auto mechanic. He liked to do things with his hands and was extraordinarily good with tools.

And John was profoundly puzzled as to the meaning and purpose of everyday, ordinary life in the light of the Gospel. It was out of his searchings, discussions, readings, and reflections that John's own sense of life's meaning and purpose grew and developed. As that growth and development took place, John's contributions to his congregation substantially changed. Through John's search and influence, many people in the congregation began to discover deeper value, meaning, and purpose for their lives in the light of the Gospel.

Some people grow and develop in this life's pilgrimage. Their contributions decisively affect the local congregation. I invite you to be thinking of the several events of internal change that are distinctive and decisive for your congregation. Think through the ways in which internal sources of change have contributed to where your congregation now is and where it is likely to be in the days and years to come.

Both external and internal changes contribute to the momentum of a congregation. We value, honor, and learn from the sources of change in our lives and in our congregation. Our momentum deepens.

THE DYNAMIC OF CONFLICT

The third dynamic that has decisive impact on the momentum of local congregations is the dynamic of conflict. There are three sources of conflict in a congregation.

> "The best of families"
> Dislocation of power
> The Gospel

"The Best of Families." The first is what I call the "best of families" conflict. Many "best of families" conflicts are honest differences of wisdom, preference, and opinion. This is true with many congregations. These conflicts grow out of our own distinctive compassion and wisdom, yearnings and longings, leanings and preferences.

With regard to preferences, some people have a preference for the color blue, some for the color green. Some persons prefer meat and some prefer fish. Some prefer the mountains and some the seashore. Some prefer music and some sports. Some prefer picnics and some movies. Some prefer games and puzzles and some prefer reading novels and mysteries. It goes on and on.

We honor one another's mutual preferences.

In deeper ways, we bring our distinctive compassion and wisdom to the major priorities in our lives and in our congregations. Some, for this time, are longing for compassion. Some are yearning for hope. Some are searching for community. We have distinctive motivations and interests.

Within congregations, we wrestle with key decisions on the strengths we have, the one or two to expand, and the one or two to add. We differ over which key objectives will help us the most. We have discussions over who will do what. We consider timing and resources. We have distinctive pictures of our future. Mostly, we discover we have much in common. Mostly, we discover a considerable consensus.

With mutual trust, respect, and integrity, we sort through these matters.

Occasionally, we find ourselves in picky and petty arguments. We are not always certain how "picky" and "petty" showed up in the discussion. We were doing all right in the discussion of some difference. We were calm. We were thoughtful. We were making headway.

Then, almost out of the blue, all of a sudden, "picky" and "petty" joined in. The more they became part of the discussion, the more "pity" showed up. Whenever "picky" and "petty" are present, "pity" is not far behind. Now, we become so preoccupied with picky, petty, and pity that we almost lose track of what we were arguing about in the first place.

Then, somehow, over the hills and dales, "the rest of the family" hears that picky, petty, and pity are having fun. They come. Anxiety shows up first. Whenever anxiety is present, fear is not far behind. Anxiety and fear breed anger. Sometimes, rage joins in.

Now, the original disagreement is virtually forgotten. Picky, petty, and pity are glad to have company. Their relatives, anxiety, fear, anger, and rage, are with them. They have not been together for a while. They are reunited. It is like old times. They go round and round the mulberry bush, holding hands, laughing and carrying on, dancing and singing, their song of conflict. They are enjoying themselves. They cannot remember when they have had so much fun.

The persons who started out discussing their disagreement are exhausted, worn out, standing almost on the sidelines, overwhelmed with what they never intended to have take place. They watch these "old friends" play out their merry games. They regret the words they have spoken. They have remorse for what they have said. They ask for forgiveness.

They say good-bye to picky, petty, pity, anxiety, fear, anger, and rage. As these "old friends" troop merrily over the hills, fading into the sunset, they do *not* say, "Come again." They hope to not see them . . . . for a long, long time. They forgive one another. They reconcile. They move on.

Yes, even in the best of families there is conflict. Even between people who deeply love one another and have lived together as husband and wife for many years, there will occasionally be a conflict. Sometimes, two sisters do not speak to one another for a period of time. They do not remember what started it. They just remember they are not speaking. At the family reunion, each is careful not to end up at the same time at the table where all the food is. They might bump into each other. They might honor that they both exist and live in this part of the galaxies. They might talk. They might forgive.

Sometimes, one brother has a tendency to beat up another brother. Sometimes, a husband and wife have been known to shout at each other. Sometimes, one brother will be at his father's house, taking the mementos that he just knows his father would want him to have, even as the other brother is at the funeral home making the arrangements for their father's funeral.

There is conflict in the best of families.

What distinguishes the best of families is their capacity for forgiveness, reconciliation, and moving on, not the absence of conflict. The only people I know who do not have conflict are the people buried in the nearest cemetery. And, sometimes, I'm not so sure about them . . . . when I walk by late at night, I hear the mutterings and the murmurings. Conflict is present in the best of families.

Sometimes we seek to model ourselves after the early church, assuming that was an idyllic and peaceful time. Read freshly Paul's letter to the church at Galatia, which had its raging conflicts. What marks the best of congregations is the congregation's capacity for forgiveness, reconciliation, and moving on, not the absence of conflict.

Dislocation of Power. The second source of conflict is the trend in our country toward dislocation of power. Over the past fifty years, power has been dislocated from local and regional sources to national and international sources. As a result, people in our time have experienced a pervasive sense of powerlessness. For many, many people, the decisions that affect their lives and shape their destinies are made somewhere else by someone else, and one cannot quite always find out whom or what or where.

We go down to the courthouse to transact a simple bit of business. We are directed to the new courthouse annex. We go to the new courthouse annex. We are directed up to the second floor, third door on the right. We visit with a pleasant gray-haired lady. She tells us that the matter used to be done there. However, it is now done at the state capital.

We write the state capital. We get a letter back that says that it used to be done there. However, it is now done in a regional office. We write the regional office. We get a letter back that says it used to be done there. However, it is now done in Washington, D.C. We write to Washington, D.C.

We get a letter back. It says that if we go down to the new courthouse annex, second floor, third door on the right, a pleasant gray-haired lady will help us. In our time, lots of people experience a profound sense of powerlessness over their lives and destinies.

The two symptoms of this sense of powerlessness are apathy and anger. I am frequently invited to help a local congregation think through the apathy of its members. It is not as simple as church apathy. If one looks closely at those persons who are expressing apathy, one discovers that in all spheres and sectors of their lives, there is a sense of apathy. We can look at all of these areas.

Human hurt and hope	Scientific
Economic	Medical
Educational	Music and arts
Societal	Recreational
Political	Environmental
Missional	Demographic
Vocational	Geographical
Religious	

Again and again, people who are leaders in these areas teach me of their frustrating, wearisome experiences with people who express apathy in their area. These leaders say to me, "Dr. Callahan, please help us to overcome the apathy we are up against."

It is not as simple as saying, "If people only had more commitment, they would not have apathy." The key is power, not commitment. The truth of the matter is, if people had more power—if people had the sense that they had more power over their own lives and destinies—then, to be sure, they would express less apathy.

Some organizations and institutions, mistakenly, have the sense that people must be lovingly controlled and coerced, pushed and directed to achieve objectives they would otherwise be unwilling to accomplish. Hearing this, some people almost fall for this way of thinking. They semi-believe it. They roll over and play dead. They live a life of apathy, not just in their church, but in most sectors and spheres of their lives.

Some groupings and congregations have the sense that people, given half of a chance, exercise initiative, self-direction, and self-control. These groupings have confidence that people have considerable creativity and imagination, that they can achieve objectives they have helped to create and for which they have ownership. In these groupings, there is considerable action and achievement. There is little apathy. They have momentum.

The second clue to this pervasive sense of powerlessness is anger. Frequently, people bring their anger with them to our congregations. They *displace* their anger in their church. Where else can they share their anger? Indeed, they have some hopes that surely in their congregation people will understand the profound roots of their anger and accept, love, and care for them, even as they express that anger.

Sometimes, in a board meeting people vent anger over the most trivial thing. Others do not always understand what is happening. Frequently, what is happening is that those people are displacing anger from some other sector of their lives in the one place they hope people will understand and accept them, namely, their church. It is a whole lot safer to shout one's anger over denominational apportionments than it is to shout one's anger over taxes and the actions of the Internal Revenue Service.

As people experience losing power in various sectors of their lives, they still count on their congregation being the one place that "when they share their wisdom or speak their piece," someone will actually listen to them . . . . that when they raise their hand and vote on something, their vote will actually count.

Sometimes, people are rightfully angry in a congregation because that congregation has lost its focus on people, service, and mission. It has become too preoccupied with money, maintenance, and membership. People have a genuine right to be angry when a congregation loses its way in this fashion. At the same time, it is important to understand that displaced anger is a clue to the pervasive sense of powerlessness many people feel in our culture.

Some church historians suggest that in the eighteenth century John Wesley saved England from the bloodbaths that were occurring across the channel during the French Revolution. They suggest that the way Wesley saved England from those bloodbaths was through the class meetings, where people, who had experienced a profound sense of powerlessness, discovered the grace of God and constructive, creative ways to recover power for the shaping of their own lives and destinies.

The Gospel. The third source of conflict is the Gospel. Now, it is *not* true that whenever there is conflict, one can automatically assume the Gospel is being shared. A few pastors make the naive, foolish mistake of assuming that simply because they are involved in conflict, they are involved in sharing the Gospel. They may, in fact, be involved in a "best of families" kind of conflict, or they may be involved in a dislocation-of-power kind of conflict. Just because it is conflict does not mean that the Gospel is being shared.

Some congregations assume that because they are weak and declining they are therefore in mission. The truth of the matter is that they are not delivering three of the five basic qualities of strong, healthy congregations. They are not delivering nine out of the twelve central characteristics. That is why they are weak and declining. They may or may not be in mission.

Some pastors assume that when the congregation is losing members it is a sign they are preaching the Gospel. Sometimes, this is the case. Sometimes, it is simply the case that the pastor is not a good shepherd. Sometimes, it is because the congregation is not delivering nine out of the twelve central characteristics. Sometimes, the pastor's preaching is inept. Sometimes, the preaching is simply displaced anger.

At the same time, it is a fact of life that the Gospel can be a source of conflict. This certainly is a part of the Biblical message. Whenever we are invited to leave off old ways and come to new ways in Christ, there will be a fair share of tension and conflict. The Gospel invites us to sort through whether the values of this world and culture are the values with which we want to live through this life's pilgrimage.

Wherever the Gospel is richly and fully preached, people will struggle with the conflict of decision as to the direction of their life and destiny. This tension is healthy. This conflict is moving. This invitation to a new life is stirring. The spirit of this conflict is decisive for people's lives and destinies. We want the nature of this conflict to be amply and fully present in our lives and in our congregation, or that congregation is no longer a congregation.

We look for and discern the sources of conflict in our congregation. We think of the several events of conflict that are distinctive and decisive for our congregation. We consider what range of conflicts are expressions of "best of families" conflicts. We sense what range of conflicts are expressions of dislocations of power. We reflect on what range of conflicts, helpfully and importantly, are expressions of the Gospel's inviting us to a new life in the grace of God. We will be insightful to the ways in which the dynamic of conflict affects our lives and our congregation. We will experience grace. We will deepen momentum.

THE DYNAMIC OF HOPE

Hope is stronger than memory.
Memory is strong.
Hope is stronger.
Hope is stronger than change.
Change is strong.
Hope is stronger.
Hope is stronger than conflict.
Conflict is strong.
Hope is stronger.

People live on hope, not on memory. Take away people's memories and they become anxious. Take away people's hopes and they become terrified. People long for and look for some sense of hope, some understanding of a reliable and certain future. Of the four dynamics, the strongest is hope.

We look for hope in the present. When we cannot see hope in the present, we look for it in the immediate future. When we cannot see hope in the immediate future, we look for hope in the distant future. When we cannot see hope in the distant future, we then look for hope in the next life future, beyond the River.

We postpone our hopes down the road. When we cannot see some hope in the present, in the immediate or in the distant future, we long for and look for some of our deepest hopes, yearnings, and longings to be fulfilled in the next life's future.

We look for sources of hope somewhere.

A few key leaders and pastors make the mistake of assuming that the art of developing an effective long-range plan is to drag people reluctantly, sometimes screamingly, from the customs, habits, and traditions of the past into the present and the

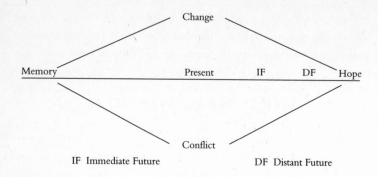

IF Immediate Future   DF Distant Future

immediate future. What these pastors and key leaders frequently
miss is that *many people are not living in the past.*

They are living in the next life future. Many people have postponed their hopes to the next life. They can see no way in which
their hopes, even some of them, will be reasonably fulfilled in the
present, immediate future, or the distant future. They are living in
the next life future.

A sociologist once did a study in Appalachia. He concluded
that the pioneers who cut down trees and built log cabins in those
early years had moved into Appalachia with a confident spirit of
hope. They saw themselves engaged in the building of a new and
promised land. But the sociologist concluded that the people who
now live in Appalachia eke out a bare, meager existence, clinging
and clutching desperately to life, and no longer share their ancestors'
sense of confident hope in the building of a new, promised land.

The one place the sociologist had failed to go was to the
white-frame, clapboard churches up the hollows and on the ridges.
These churches are surrounded by patches of country grass,
with some wildflowers, and the family cemetery near. He
missed, on Sunday morning, listening to the hymns being
sung there . . . . "We Shall Gather at the River," "In the Sweet
By-and-By," "Dwelling in Beulah Land." People postpone their
hopes. When people cannot see the fulfillment of some of
their hopes in the present, the immediate future, or the distant
future, they postpone their hopes to their next life future.

I have good friends all across the South. Some of my friends there used to sing the song, "We Shall Overcome," in a "Sweet By-and-By" way. Then, they began to sing the song in marching ways, *We Shall Overcome,* counting on, looking forward to some of their deepest hopes being fulfilled in the present and immediate future, not just in the distant and next life's future.

One clear source of resentment between some people is: some groupings have a confident spirit that some of their hopes will be realized in the present and immediate future, and some groupings see no way for any of their hopes to be realized now, or even in the immediate or distant future. Resentfully, they sometimes ask, "How can some persons have the audacity to assume that some of their hopes will be fulfilled in the present and immediate future? We see no way forward."

People live on hope, not on memory.

At the Bethlehem Church, on a Sunday morning, Mrs. Lott and I were standing out on the front porch of the church. Most of the people had gone. It hadn't taken that long. There weren't that many people to have gone. She said to me, "Dr. Callahan, I hope you will help us find a preacher who will bring us spiritual food." I listened. She went on. What she was saying was that her husband had retired from the farm and was rambling about the old farmhouse, not knowing what to do from one day to the next. Her mother was ill and dying of cancer in a nearby nursing home.

There were now strange, new kinds of people, living up and down Flowery Springs Road. They stayed up past ten o'clock at night. They wore clothes she had never seen before. One or two of them had motorcycles. What she was saying was that the sources of hope that had given her a spirit of confidence and assurance were no longer working for her .... that the hope with which she had made sense of life for the past twenty plus years were no longer working for her.

She went on to say, "I make every decision based on whether it will help me be with God in the next life." This is not a "past-based" view of life. This is a "future-based" view of life. She longed for a pastor who would help her to make some sense out of her present, everyday life with a spirit of hope for the present and the immediate future, not simply the next life future.

The New Liberty Church is in open, rural, rolling country, with farms and families, crossroads and country stores. In October, the fields and trees, the creeks and ponds are beautiful to behold. One day, the kids rode their horses across the church cemetery. People got upset. People got upset not simply because they thought the horses and the kids were desecrating the ancestors of the past. People got upset because the horses and the kids were trampling on the church's symbol of the future. The church cemetery is not a symbol of the past.

We know those who are buried there are not really there. We only fix the cemetery up once a year, just before homecoming. We want to be buried there not so we can lie beside so-and-so, but because our cemetery is the symbol of each family's entrance into the kingdom of hope beyond this life. To be sure, our cemetery honors those who have gone before. But most important, the focus is on where they have gone—to a new and promised land, the land of hope.

We want to be buried there because our cemetery is a symbol of hope for the future. Many congregations across the planet have a homecoming each year. Church homecomings are not events that look to the past only. Church homecomings are events that look to the future. The homecoming is a present-day, proleptic event that looks to the great homecoming "beyond the River" when we will all be gathered as God's family.

Some persons find themselves drawn to churches that preach quaint, nonsensical, foolish apocalyptic understandings of the future. These persons are desperately searching for some sense of hope. However quaint, nonsensical, foolish, and apocalyptic the promise of hope is in that congregation, at least it has the echo of hope about it.

Too many of our congregations have services of worship that conclude on the cross. Too many of our congregations have services of worship that include sermons with a fifteen- to eighteen-minute problem analysis and a quick, closing generality that "Jesus is the answer." Most people know their problems reasonably well. What people come to a church longing and looking for is a sense of help, a sense of home, and a sense of hope. People are drawn even to those congregations that only promise a tawdry sense of hope.

Nostalgia is not a retreat to the past. Nostalgia is looking back to a time when some of our deepest hopes, longings, and yearnings were fulfilled. We draw that picture forward as the only picture of the future to which we can cling, because no clearer picture seems available to us. We are all wise enough to know that Grover's Corners is no more. To be sure, it may exist now here, now there, in some hidden valley not yet discovered in the first half of the twenty-first century. Mostly, the "Our Towns" of our planet, like the town in Thornton Wilder's play *Our Town,* are no more.

There, everybody went to bed at ten o'clock at night, and the train went through about the same time every night. There, Emily and George married. They began a quiet life together. But, even in Grover's Corners, Emily died in childbirth. Grover's Corners is no more. Nostalgia is an effort to put before us some picture of hope when no other picture of hope seems possible.

I have helped many congregations frozen on the face of a cliff. Think about mountain climbing. Think about what it is like to find oneself on the face of a cliff where one cannot reach the handholds and footholds ahead, and one cannot get back to the handholds and footholds one has left behind.

What do we do in this predicament? We do one thing extraordinarily well. We freeze to the face of the cliff. We cling and clutch for dear life. We want no movement. The only movement we can see is the abyss below. Some congregations are like this. They can find no handholds and footholds of the past to go back to, and they can find no handholds and footholds for the future. They cling and clutch for dear life to the face of the cliff and freeze, immobile, desiring no change.

You and I, frozen to the face of the cliff, would not want very much change either. And then, some cheery person comes along at the safety of the top of the cliff and hollers down instructions in a loud voice, "Oh, it is simple! Just do as I tell you." You and I know what happens next. Frozen to the face of the cliff, we are disrupted, alarmed even more. We lose our handholds and footholds and fall into the abyss below. Or, what mostly happens, we cling and clutch even tighter and, more desperately, want no change.

When a person is frozen to the face of a cliff, we join him or her on the face of the cliff. Gently and quietly, we coach the person forward. Here is this handhold. Here is this foothold. Now, here is another handhold. Now, here is this foothold. And sometimes, gently and quietly, inch by inch, we coach the person forward to new handholds and footholds. The same is true of congregations. Helpful leaders gently and quietly coach their congregation forward to new handholds and new footholds.

Two things are true about the kingdom. The kingdom has come. The kingdom is coming. The reality of the kingdom has happened. The fulfillment of the kingdom is before us. The kingdom is now here, now there. The kingdom "happens" in every event of reconciliation, wholeness, caring, and justice. The kingdom "happens" in every event of grace . . . . every event of compassion . . . . every event of community . . . . every event of hope. These events are proleptic experiences of the kingdom. Where grace is, there is the kingdom.

Hope and living are good friends. Hope and planning are good friends. There is direct correlation between hope and living. There is direct correlation between hope and planning. What is helpful in many congregations is a theology of hope . . . . a profound, rich, full theology of hope. Hope and planning go hand in hand. One cannot do one without the other. Our theology of hope gives us confidence and assurance for the present and the future. We live in grace. We live in hope.

Some church groupings have virtually no rich, full theology of hope. They have given the field over to sectarian, quaint apocalyptic understandings of eschatology that are nonsensical and foolish. When church groupings abandon a rich, full eschatology, they are in a weaker position to do effective planning. Hope informs planning. Planning informs hope. The two go hand in hand. In our time, we benefit from the development of a richer, fuller, more profound theology of hope that takes seriously the dynamics of conflict, change, and memory.

Sometimes, you and I are the Flimsies People. Think of an overhead projector. In some parts of the planet, the sheet we write on is called a transparency. In some parts of the planet, it is called a flimsy. A flimsy is transparent. You can see through it. It bends easily. It has little substance.

There are times when people are drawn to flimsies. You and I vest our hopes in the flimsies of this life . . . . the new car, the new house, the new trinket, the new gadget, the new this or that. The list of flimsies is amazing. And, the new car is a source of hope until it gets its first scratch. We move on to the next flimsy of hope.

We share and work with persons in our congregations and communities who see their primary sources of hope in the flimsies of this life. You and I are sometimes part of the Flimsies People.

We share and work with persons in our congregations and communities who are the Cliff People. You and I find ourselves, on occasion, part of the Cliff People. We see no way forward. We see no way behind. We freeze.

We share and work with persons who are the River People. They, and we, vest our hopes in the next life, beyond the River. The art with Mrs. Lott is to help her discover sources of hope in the distant future, the immediate future, and the present, not just the next life future beyond the River. It is not a matter of dragging her from the past. She is not there. She is living, with her hopes on the other side of the River. Sometimes, we do too.

When we live life well, we are the Easter People. We are the People of Hope. We practice, in our praying, planning, and living, a spirit of hope in the grace of God.

I have been in church after church where the Sunday morning bulletins share the names of the sick and dying. During the time of prayer concerns, people speak out to say for whom they would like to pray. Inevitably, those prayer concerns focus on the sick and dying. This teaches every person gathered there, including every first-time visitor, that this is primarily a sick and dying congregation.

I was with one congregation at a special Sunday morning service of remembrance. Printed in the church bulletin were the names of every person who had died during the previous year. At the appropriate time in the service, the pastor read each name slowly and lovingly. The congregation bell tolled in the background. The organ played gently. A helpful prayer of triumph followed. We sang a strong hymn of celebration for the dead, for who they had been with us, for who they are with us, and for who they are with God. It was a moving, meaningful service.

After the service, the pastor asked me what I thought. I told him the service was most helpful. And then I said to him, "When do you do the same service for those people who have been born this past year? When do you do the same for those people who are celebrating a major accomplishment and achievement in their own lives? When do you do the same for persons who have discovered new life in the grace of God this year?"

We want the help of prayer when we are ill or dying. But life is not a matter of sickness and death only. Life is also a matter of grace and compassion, community and hope. Our prayer life can have a spirit of balance. We pray earnestly for persons who experience tragic, traumatic events and times of illness and death. We pray earnestly for persons who experience times of joy and celebration, new life and hope.

You can ask yourself the extent to which your services of worship have this balance. Strong, healthy congregations tend to celebrate their service of worship on the first day of the week. The grassroots, the pastor, the choir director, the worship leaders, the ushers, the greeters of newcomers, and the key leaders of the congregation understand that this service of worship begins the week to come. Whenever I find this spirit, I tend to find a well-prepared service of worship. It has the qualities of integrity and spontaneity, of compassion and hope. I tend to find a service that launches the week to come with expectancy and a sense of excitement.

By contrast, whenever I find a weak and declining congregation, I tend to find a congregation where worship is seen as happening on the last day of the week, not the first. If you think your week begins on Monday morning at your job, your worship is occurring on the last day of the week. Some pastors make the mistake of thinking their work week begins on Monday morning in the office rather than on Sunday in worship with the congregation. Whenever pastors and key leaders think of worship as occurring on the last day of the week, two things happen.

First, worship becomes less well prepared. It is the leftover event, the last thing done in the week. We get so caught up in the busyness of the week. We get to worship last. The service tends to look back on what has been. It tends to summarize the week that has been rather than look forward to the week that will be. For the week that has been, we can ask God's forgiveness for our sins and shortcomings. We can thank God for the gifts and strengths with which God has blessed us this past week. But, we cannot change what has been.

Deepen your momentum. Look forward to celebrating worship on the first day of the week. Whenever a pastor and congregation see the week beginning with worship on the first day of the week, there is a sense of expectancy, hope, and momentum in the congregation. Of the four dynamics that affect the present and future of a congregation: memory, change, conflict, and hope . . . . the strongest is hope.

We are not a people of the cross only. Some congregations become preoccupied with the cross only. They are trapped on the cross. They think of themselves on the cross, sick and dying only. They live only a portion of the Gospel. Yes, life is sickness and death. But there is more to the good news than simply the cross.

A group of women walked to a tomb on the first day of the week. We are a first-day people. The Open Tomb is stronger than the bloodied cross. The Risen Lord is stronger than the dead Jesus. Easter is stronger than Good Friday. We are the people of the Open Tomb, the Risen Lord, and New Life in Christ. We are the People of Hope. We are the Easter People. We are the People of Grace.

Five qualities contribute to your momentum. Begin with motivation. Grow as persons achieve key objectives. Develop power with an effective long-range plan. Move forward as you discover the value of excellent mistakes. Move forward as you recognize some objectives are worth not doing. Deepen your value of memory, change, conflict, and hope. God will bless you with momentum. God will bless you with grace.

Part Two

RESOURCES

6

CONGREGATION, COMMUNITY, DIRECTION

THE PERSONS OUR CONGREGATION SERVES

One of your major resources is the total persons your congregation serves.

Most congregations serve more people than they think they do. Developing a sense of the total persons you serve will benefit you and your congregation. You can share this information in a study session prior to your **Twelve Keys Celebration Retreat.** You can share the information during the retreat, or you can share it following your celebration retreat as further encouragement for your congregation.

Most congregations serve more persons than they think they do.

Most congregations serve five groupings of people:

1. *Persons served in mission*—we deliver direct help with their human hopes and hurts, in the grace of God and on behalf of the congregation. There is a direct relationship between these persons and some persons in our congregation. Hospital visits, community mission projects, funerals, weddings, and shepherding emergencies are examples.

2. *Constituents*—nonmembers who participate in one or more activities. Congregations have far more constituents than they are aware of. Constituents participate in worship

on Christmas Eve, Christmas, Easter, and on other major
Sundays. Constituents participate in Vacation Bible School,
recreation leagues, quilting groups, preschool, and so on.
All children who are not yet members are constituents.
Constituents frequently think of themselves as members. It
is an "informal" understanding of membership.

3. *Members*—resident members who are marginally active
to fully active in the life of the congregation. Nonresident
members and inactive members are not included in this
grouping.

4. *Community persons*—persons in the local community
who think well of your congregation and its mission.
They share generous support with the congregation as it
serves in some distinctive mission in the community. Their
spirit is to support worthwhile mission projects.

5. *Friends of the congregation who live elsewhere*—these
persons grew up in the congregation and, now, for various
reasons, live elsewhere. Or, they moved to the community and found home with the congregation. Time passed.
They were transferred in their work to another community. They still view this congregation as home. They hope
to return one day.

The art is to discover where you are now in the total number of people your congregation serves. Most local congregations
serve more people than they think they do. Some people think of
their congregation primarily in terms of how many members—
50, 140, 300, 500, 700 members—it has. The *best* way to think of
your congregation is in terms of the *total number of persons served*.

I was helping a congregation. I asked the group how many
members they had. They indicated they had 500 members. Then
I asked, "How many constituents do you have?" As they thought
about it, they could think of 450 constituents who were a part
of the life of their congregation.

Next, I asked, "How many people does your congregation
serve in mission in a year's time?" A *person served in mission* is a
nonmember or a nonconstituent in the local community who

is directly helped with a specific human hurt, and that help-ing is directly linked to your congregation. They could think of approximately 200 persons in the local community whom their congregation had helped in some way during the previ-ous year.

Then, I asked about friends of the congregation who live elsewhere. They thought there were 100. I asked about commu-nity persons. They could think about 150.

Then, I asked the group, "What is the total number of people your congregation serves?" There was silence in the group. Quietly, someone suggested, "Well, we have 500 members." The group shushed the person. Several said, almost at once, with gentle smiles on their faces, "We serve 1,400 persons." The group had a spirit of generous amazement. They had not real-ized the total persons they are serving.

I said to the group, "Your whole congregational family is 1,400 persons. God blesses you with a rich, full family."

Some congregations focus on the question, "How many leaders and staff members should we have in relation to our member-ship?" That is an interesting question, but not very helpful. A better focus would be, "How many leaders and staff members are helpful in relation to the total persons served in this congregation?"

Many congregations have deep compassion for people. They share generous service. They advance their strengths. They have key leaders, volunteers, and staff in relation to the total number of people served. In the previous example, the total number of peo-ple served would be fourteen hundred persons. To use the medi-cal term, this is the total patient load. To use the missional term, this is the total mission load . . . . the total number of people served by this congregation in a given year.

In our current mission culture, people are likely, first, to be persons served in mission. Then, some of them decide to become constituents. Then, some constituents decide to be members . . . . to become part of the mission.

In our current mission culture, many community persons are glad to help with a major project your congregation is doing—that will directly benefit the community. Most congregations have direct "linkages" with many community persons. People in your congregation have relationships with many persons in these community networks:

friendship
common interests
life stage
human hurt and hope
vocational
recreational
music and arts

Community persons both volunteer and give generously to a worthwhile major project for two reasons:

1. They value the people in the community who will be helped.
2. They know and respect someone in the congregation.

Strong, healthy congregations have a helpful focus with persons served in mission. This is where we live in our time. Those congregations who work on membership only are limiting their abilities to serve. In our time, the objective is not on the number of new members we get. The objective is on the number of persons we serve in mission in a year. We do not focus on member growth. We focus on mission growth.

With the following Figure 6.1, you can discover the total persons you are currently serving.

Most congregations discover they serve more persons than they thought they do. You can decide which of these five groupings you would have fun drawing more fully into the life of your congregation and its mission. You can decide which of these five grouping you would like to grow in the future.

Mission congregations tend to focus on growing the first grouping, persons served in mission. In a bygone time, congregations would set membership objectives. That was in a church culture. In a mission culture. we set persons served in mission

	Current Estimated Number	Future Objective
Persons Served in Mission persons helped through our congregation's mission, in the recent five years, or at some point in the past	_____	_____
Constituents nonmembers who participate in some mission, shepherding, worship, grouping, or activity of your congregation	_____	_____
Members resident members marginally active to fully active.	_____	_____
Community Persons persons in the local community who share generous support with the congregation's distinctive mission in the community.	_____	_____
Friends of the Congregation who live elsewhere persons grew up in the congregation, live elsewhere moved to the community, found home, transferred, still view as home	_____	_____
Total Persons Our Congregation Serves	_____	_____

Figure 6.1 Total Persons Served

objectives. We look forward to serving _____ (fill in the future objective) persons served in mission.

One of your major resources is the total number of persons in your congregational family.

THE PERSONS OUR CONGREGATION CAN SERVE

One of your major resources is the total persons your congregation can serve. Most congregations can serve more people than they think they can. Developing a sense of the total persons you can serve will benefit you and your congregation.

You can help your congregation discover your maximum mission potential. Most congregations have a stronger maximum mission potential than they are aware of. Many are still acting as though it were the church culture of the 1950s. Regrettably, some congregations have a mission statement that sounds like the nursery rhyme about Little Bo Peep: "Leave them alone and they'll come home . . . ."

These congregations live under the myth that when young couples have their first baby they will be back at church. This does sometimes happen—just enough times in a decade to make the myth believable, when in fact it is a myth.

Congregations also perpetuate the myth that newcomers if they want a congregation "know where we are; let them find us." There are just enough newcomers who do come into a congregation to visit during a decade to make them believe this, when in fact it is a myth. This is one of the richest mission fields on this planet. It is most helpful for your congregation to discover its maximum mission potential.

Then, you can decide how far you want to go—that is, you can think through your objective as to the number of new people you will serve in mission in each year of your long-range plan . . . . the first year, the second year, the third year, and so on.

Most congregations can serve more persons than they think they can.

You can use the worksheet in Figure 6.2, the Maximum Mission Potential Formula, to discover the range of persons your congregation can serve. These basic points help.

Average trip time (ATT) is the amount of time people invest in traveling to work, doing major shopping, going to school, and participating in major social and recreational activities. Average trip time does not refer to the amount of time people invest in driving to a congregation. Rather, it refers to the amount of time people spend in everyday life in an average trip. People measure trips in minutes, not miles. People develop an average "trip time horizon." Communities have "trip time horizons."

In metropolitan areas, the average trip time is thirty minutes or more. In small towns, the average trip time may be five to ten minutes. In rural areas, the average trip time may be forty-five minutes to an hour. People invest, in driving to church, the same average trip time as they do in everyday life.

The total population within the average trip time radius of your congregation is your primary mission field. A congregation can be in mission with the hurts and hopes that are present within that total population. We do consider the geographical barriers, community boundaries, and major traffic patterns that influence our capacity to be in mission with given groups of people.

Significant geographical barriers (SGB) are rivers, mountains, major expressways, and so on. *Community boundaries (CB)* are the visible and invisible boundaries that shape the direction and pattern of people's lives. For example, a dotted line on a map indicates the line between Morgan County and Smith County. People live on either side of that dotted line. It is a strong community boundary.

Traffic directional patterns (TDP) are the way people move about in day-to-day life. People tend to go to church along the traffic patterns they follow in the course of an ordinary week. People who drive from north to south to work, with an average trip time of twenty minutes, are more likely to drive from north to south to a congregation that is located twenty minutes from their house.

They are less likely to drive the opposite direction, from south to north, to a congregation that is only ten minutes from their house. There are exceptions to this basic principle, but, again and again, people tend to live out their lives in regular traffic direction patterns.

With regard to our congregation's maximum mission potential, we want to be realistic as to the number of people available with which we can be in mission.

In sparsely populated areas such as West Texas or the Outback of Australia, for example, the maximum mission potential may be only forty persons who are unchurched within a one-hour driving time. There are lots of cattle and cactus, scorpions and snakes, kangaroos and dingoes—and very few people.

	Now	Projected Ten Years Ahead
1. Compute the average trip time (ATT) in your community.	———	———
2. Calculate the total population with in ATT radius of your congregation.	———	———
3. Adjust for significant geographical barriers, community boundaries, and major traffic directional patterns.	———	———
4. Calculate 60% of the adjusted total population from step 3 to discover unchurched population within ATT of your congregation.	———	———

4.   Use 70% or 80% when there is a greater density of unchurched population.

| 5. Compute 20% of unchurched population from step 4 to discover homogeneous potential for mission. | ——— | ——— |

5.   Use 25% for homogeneous areas of the the country and 15% for heterogeneous areas.

| 6. For your realistic Maximum Mission Potential, increase the homogeneous unchurched population figure from step 5 by 20% based on the principle of heterogeneity. | ——— | ——— |

6.   Use 30% when the congregation has extraordinary compassion and a substantial

Figure 6.2 Maximum Mission Potential

Most congregations are not in West Texas or the Outback. They have considerable mission potential. Our planet is one of the richest mission fields ever. God has placed us in a major age of mission. God invites us to be good shepherds in this time and place.

In step 4, the formula invites you to adjust the total population figure by 60 percent. In some areas, with a higher proportion of unchurched people, adjust the total population figure by 70 or 80 percent, depending on the number of unchurched people in the community.

In step 5, for computing the homogeneous potential, use 20 percent. For more homogeneous populations, you can use 25 percent. For more heterogeneous areas, you can use a 15 percent figure. The principle of homogeneity is helpful. The principle of mission heterogeneity is more helpful.

God invites us to serve in mission. Hence, we compute step 6. We increase the figure in step 5 by 20 percent. Increase the figure by 30 percent wherever two factors are present: (1) the congregation has an extraordinary compassion for mission in the community, and (2) a substantial percentage of the community is unchurched.

You can share this information in a study session prior to your actual **Twelve Keys Celebration Retreat.** You can share the information during the retreat, or you can share it following your celebration retreat as further encouragement for your congregation.

You now know the maximum mission potential of your congregation. Consider how many new people you can realistically hope to serve in your community each year .... persons you are not now serving, persons you will seek out, persons you can help with specific human hurts and hopes.

The step of selecting a mission objective is a new venture for many congregations. The setting of a mission objective invites your congregation to be self-giving rather than self-seeking and self-serving. Since the church culture days of the 1950s, congregations have set objectives year after year with respect to the number of new members they plan to reach, the increase in worship attendance they hope to achieve, and the number of church school enrollments they hope to accomplish.

Rarely have congregations thought through a specific mission objective as to the number of new people whom they look forward to reaching in mission during the coming year. Simply setting this mission objective honors the fact that this is a new day—we are, in fact, on a mission field in our time.

I'm not proposing that a congregation try to serve its full maximum mission potential in the first year of its long-range plan. Depending on the size of the maximum mission potential available to a given congregation, it would be a reasonable objective for a congregation to seek to serve 5 to 10 to 15 percent of the total maximum mission potential in the first year of an effective long-range plan.

God encourages us to be a mission congregation.

THE PRIMARY DIRECTION OUR CONGREGATION IS HEADING

The resource in Figure 6.3 will benefit you and your congregation. Some congregations do not know where they are heading.

Develop the primary direction for your congregation's future.
This primary direction entails decisions regarding:

1. The total number of persons your
   congregation serves now: _____
   Members, constituents, persons served in
   mission, community persons, and friends
   of our congregation who live elsewhere

2. The maximum mission potential available   _____
   to you in your community
   See Figure 6.2

3. The total number of persons your congregation
   plans to serve in the coming
   year . . . . three years . . . . or five years
       this year _____ three years _____   five years _____

   You can decide the primary direction for your
   congregation.

Figure 6.3 The Primary Direction for Our Congregation

They are dying congregations. Some almost know where they are heading. They are weak and declining. Strong, healthy congregations know where they are heading.

Many congregations are mission growth congregations. Many, many congregations are deciding to be mission growth congregations. Some congregations decide to be weak, declining congregations. Some decide to be dying congregations.

What I say next may not apply in West Texas or the Outback of Australia, both of which I dearly love, but there are comparatively few people living in either region. Most everywhere else, there are considerable numbers of people living in the area, most of whom are unchurched.

Some congregations set membership objectives for the number of new members they plan to get in the coming year, three years, and five years.

You are welcome to set mission objectives for the number of persons your congregation plans to serve in the coming year, three years, and five years.

Mission growth congregations begin with the question of mission.

The question is: Who is God inviting us to serve in mission?
　　Do we want to be a serving congregation?
The question is not: Do we want to be a growing congregation?
　　Do we want to grow?
We serve for the sake of serving. We do not serve to grow.
　　We share mission for the sake of mission.
　　We do not do mission to grow.
The goal is serving, not growing. When we serve, sometimes we grow.
　　Then, we give thanks to God twice, first for the serving and, second, for the new persons who have joined with us in the serving.
There is some correlation.

The more persons we serve in mission, the more persons who become part of our mission. Some are persons we now serve in mission who, later, want to be part of serving in our mission. Some are persons in the community who want to serve in our mission.

We have these resources: congregation, community, and direction. God blesses us with a wondrous world of mission.

7

POSSIBILITIES

THE FOUR INVITATIONAL QUESTIONS

We discover possibilities for our future with these four invitational questions. These invitational questions open us to:

Experiencing the grace of God
Discovering the possibilities to which God is inviting us
Developing a whole, healthy life

These four questions are important in developing both a strong, healthy congregation and a whole, healthy life. I encourage you to hold these four invitational questions before yourself and the group as you develop your long-range plan.

The four invitational questions are:

Where are we headed?
What kind of future are we building?
What are our strengths, gifts, and competencies?
Who is God inviting us to serve in mission?

I encourage you to share the content and the spirit of these invitational questions with your whole congregation as you develop your long-range plan.

I call these questions *invitational* because they are intended to encourage your reflection and foster your sense of direction.

They are not questions intended to be answered on the front end of a long-range planning process with definite precision and conclusive finality. Do not invest extraordinary amounts of time developing precise answers to these four invitational questions.

Rather, invitational questions are those that you and your congregation keep in mind as you move toward developing an effective long-range plan. The questions have a drawing, leading, invitational character. They are the kind of questions to be kept ever before you as you seek to discern, with compassion, wisdom, judgment, vision, common sense, and prayer, the future direction that will be most helpful for your congregation.

Life is a pilgrimage. In developing a long-range plan you are deciding the specific direction of your congregation's pilgrimage in mission for the years to come. This processive, dynamic, developmental, invitational character of long-range planning is important for leaders to understand and share early in the planning process. When the planning has been completed, ask these four invitational questions again—they are still leading you.

The Future Toward Which We Are Headed. The first question, "Where are we headed?" confirms that we can look to the future. The wrong first question would have been, "Where have we been?" That would have invited us to look to the past. The congregation that looks to the past does not see God. Yes, we can discover the nature of God's acts of grace in the past. These are helpful to know.

God is not in the past. God has acted decisively and compassionately, powerfully and gently in the past. And, God has moved on to the present and to the future. This is where God's acts of grace are happening now.

The most decisive understanding of God in the Old Testament is of the God who goes before the people as a cloud by day and a fire by night, leading them toward the future God has both promised and prepared. The most decisive understanding of God in the New Testament is of the Open Tomb, the Risen Lord, and New Life in Christ.

The congregation that looks to the future sees God. God goes before your congregation, inviting your congregation to that future which God has both promised and is preparing for you. The question, "Where are we headed?" confirms we can take up this invitation.

The Future We Are Building. What kind of future are we building for our families . . . . our community . . . . our world . . . . our congregation? This is the proper order and sequence for the second question. Something far more important is at stake in developing an effective long-range plan than the simple survival of a given local congregation.

Effective long-range planning is concerned with the lives and destinies of your families, your friends, and the many, many people who will be helped by your congregation in the years to come.

Effective long-range planning is concerned with the character and quality of life in the community. There is a direct correlation between the strength of the strongest congregations in a community and the character and quality of life in that community. The stronger the strongest congregations in the community, the stronger the character and quality of life in that community.

Effective long-range planning has at stake the spirit of mission and compassion, peace and justice, value and betterment of our world. We are mission congregations, and we have a deep compassion for the world.

Effective long-range planning has at stake the future direction and advancement of our congregation. What rides on effective long-range planning is not something as simple as the survival of a local congregation. Indeed, those congregations that focus their long-range planning on the survival of their congregation are those congregations that have decided to die.

God invites us to a theology of service, not a theology of survival. It is regrettable that some congregations get caught up in long-range planning to survive. We can move beyond a preoccupation with the three M's—maintenance, money, and membership. Congregations that do the best job of long-range planning are those congregations that live a theology of service, not survival, mission, not maintenance.

These congregations see that what is at stake, that what rides on developing an effective long-range plan are the lives and destinies of many, many families, the character and quality of life in the community, the sense of reconciliation, justice, and peace in our world, and the advancement and betterment in mission of a local congregation.

Our Strengths, Gifts, and Competencies. The third invitational question is, "What are our strengths, gifts, and competencies?" The congregation that claims its strengths claims God. The congregation that claims its strengths claims God's gifts. I am not inviting you to a naive, foolish optimism or a whistling-in-the-dark positive thinking. Rather, I am inviting you to a Biblically based, God-centered understanding of life—and of effective long-range planning.

The congregation that claims its strengths claims the ways in which God has been living and moving and stirring among this congregation for many years. We are who we are, with what strengths, gifts, and competencies we have, as gifts from God.

The congregation that denies its strengths denies God. The person who denies his or her strengths denies God's gifts. In life's pilgrimage some people suffer from low self-esteem, thinking more poorly of themselves than they have a right to, looking down on themselves. They deny God. They deny God's gifts. Likewise, some congregations suffer from low self-esteem and think more poorly of themselves than they have a right to. They look down on themselves. They deny God. They deny God's gifts.

Some congregations have excellent, experienced pro players at center, right guard, right tackle, right end, and right halfback. They develop a long-range plan that runs around a weak left end. Some congregations have excellent, experienced pro leaders in certain central characteristics of an effective congregation. They design a long-range plan to focus on their shortcomings and concerns. They focus on their weaknesses rather than building on their strengths.

The art of long-range planning is to build on your strengths. Do better what you do best. Then . . . . you are in a stronger position to tackle your weaknesses and shortcomings.

The four worst "best questions" to consider in developing an effective long-range plan are these:

What are our problems?
What are our needs?
What are our concerns?
What are our weaknesses and shortcomings?

Some congregations go off on a retreat each year with enough newsprint to wallpaper three walls. They begin their planning by inviting everyone in the room to list their congregation's problems, needs, concerns, weaknesses, and shortcomings. During the first few hours of the planning retreat they successfully fill three walls of newsprint listing 114 problems, needs, concerns, weaknesses, and shortcomings. They accomplish three things: a rich, full harvest of despair; a rich, full harvest of depression; and a rich, full harvest of despondency.

Why do some congregations do this? Some pastors and key leaders are attracted to those four questions. They have their own sense of despair, depression, and despondency. This is understandable, from time to time, when someone is engaged in something as complex, difficult, and ambiguous as being in mission on one of the richest mission fields on the planet.

Some pastors and key leaders seem attracted, as moths to the flame, to those four worst "best questions." After listing 114 problems, needs, concerns, weaknesses, and shortcomings, everybody else in the room has their own full share of despair, depression, and despondency. Now, the despondent pastors and key leaders don't feel quite as bad because everybody else feels a whole lot worse. Misery does sometimes love company.

I have been frequently invited to help congregations teetering on the brink of the abyss, almost ready to fall into the depths of the chasm below. I am not proposing we deny or never examine problems, needs, concerns, weaknesses, and shortcomings. It is simply the case that a congregation that first claims its strengths is in a stronger position to deal with its shortcomings.

A congregation that begins long-range planning with the four worst best questions becomes preoccupied with its problems. It becomes distracted. It doesn't see its strengths well enough to build them forward in order to become stronger and, thereby, move into a better position to tackle its problems, needs, concerns, weaknesses, and shortcomings.

I call these four worst "best questions" the four horsemen of the apocalypse—the four assassins of hope. They lead a congregation to begin its long-range planning process without God. They lead a congregation to begin its long-range planning process without recognizing and giving thanks for God's gifts.

The third invitational question is decisive because it helps a congregation begin its long-range planning process by claiming the ways in which God has been living and moving and stirring in this congregation for many years. Whatever strengths, gifts, and competencies we have, we have as God's gifts. We, therefore, begin our long-range planning with God.

God's Encouraging Invitation to Mission. The fourth invitational question is, "Who is God inviting us to serve in mission?" You will note that the question does not ask what we want to do. Fortunately, some earlier approaches to long-range planning are now virtually archeological relics. The old "I wish," or "I dream," approach and the "If you had one million dollars, how would you spend it?" approach have nearly faded from the scene.

The failure of these approaches is that they all begin with "I." What is decisive in long-range planning is: Who is *God* inviting us to serve in mission? It takes compassion, wisdom, judgment, vision, common sense, and prayer to discern the nature of God's invitation to your congregation in the coming three, five, or seven years.

You will note a second implication. The question clearly asks, Who is God inviting us to *serve*? The focus of the question is on serving, not on activities and doings. We are not living the myth of the busy, bustling suburban congregation of the church culture of the 1950s, where the task of the congregation seemed to be to help people become busily involved in a merry-go-round of doings and activities. After all that busyness, many congregations looked back after several years and wondered what they had accomplished and achieved on behalf of God's mission.

Effective long-range planning focuses on God's invitation to accomplish and achieve on behalf of God's mission. The term *mission,* you will note, is the third decisive characteristic of this question. The question asks, Who is God inviting us to serve in *mission*? The question is not, What is God calling us to accomplish in ministry?

Unfortunately, the term *ministry* has acquired the false connotation that the "real work" of the congregation is being done by the ordained clergy. Further, the term *ministry* suggests a connotation that we are still living in the church culture of the 1950s. The truth of the matter is that this is one of the richest mission fields on the planet.

We go to a door and knock on it. Someone comes to the door and says, "Oh, well, we're Presbyterian." We know immediately they are effectively unchurched. If they had come to the door and said, "Oh, we go to First Presbyterian; Dr. Smith is our pastor," we know they are churched. Whenever a person shares with us primarily a denominational label, we can usually count on that person being effectively unchurched. They are teaching us either the church of their childhood memories or the church where they have an affiliation and are not active.

Dr. George Morris, who served as a distinguished professor of evangelism at Candler School of Theology, Emory University, a wonderful pastor, and a good friend, once told me of the eight months he lived in central Appalachia. He spent much of that time visiting families, knocking on doors up and down the hollows, ridges, and valleys. Seventy percent of the families he visited were effectively unchurched.

Many of those families could not even remember anyone in their family who, in their living memory, had been Christian—an aunt, a grandfather, a great uncle, or a great grandmother. I was in Ohio helping a congregation, and the pastor mentioned to me the fact that he was formerly a missionary in Africa. I said to him, "Yes, you were a former missionary in Africa. Now, my good friend, you are currently a missionary—in Ohio."

Who is God inviting . . . . calling us to serve in mission? God invites us to see that the day of mission is at hand. Those congregations that continue to behave as though this were the church culture of the 1950s will do one thing predictably well—they will become weak and declining or dying congregations.

Many congregations have discovered that we live on one of the richest mission fields on earth. They are reaching out, on behalf of the grace of God, to serve the human hurts and hopes of the countless hundreds upon hundreds of people who live within average trip time of where their congregation gathers each Sunday morning.

QUALITIES

These qualities help us discover possibilities for our future:

> Compassion
> Wisdom
> Judgment
> Vision
> Common sense
> Prayer

Long-range planning is an art, not a skill. Long-range planning invites the best *mutual* compassion, wisdom, judgment, vision, common sense, and prayer of all the participants. These are the major qualities people bring with them as the congregation develops its future. As you draw on these major qualities, you share in developing an effective long-range plan that will help you move forward.

Effective long-range planning is not finally a matter of gimmicks and gadgets, graphs and charts, tricks and trivialities, the latest data and demographics. Sometimes, when I have been asked, "What are the major qualities for developing a long-range plan?" the question has had an implicit corollary, "Is there some neat and nifty, quick and easy gimmick someone could learn?" Effective long-range planning is not that simplistic.

Central to developing an effective long-range plan is the 20–80 principle: 20 percent of the things a group does yields 80 percent of its results, accomplishments, and achievements. Conversely, 80 percent of what a group does yields 20 percent of its results. Two out of ten plays win football games. The art is in selecting the best two plays.

Of one hundred things your congregation will work on in the coming three to five years, twenty will deliver 80 percent of the future for your congregation. Focus on the 20 percenters that will yield 80 percent of the results.

Discerning which objectives are the 20 percenters, among all those you could do, requires considerable compassion, wisdom, judgment, vision, common sense, and prayer.

The myth in some congregations is, "If people were only more committed and worked harder, things would get better." The truth is that when people work harder, they get tireder. Things don't necessarily get better. When a person who is digging a hole for himself or herself works harder, he or she simply digs a deeper hole. When a congregation, headed in the wrong direction, works harder, it simply goes in the wrong direction quicker and faster .... and gets more tired in the process.

The art is to work smarter, not harder. Focus only on those 20 percenters that will deliver 80 percent of the future. In the long term, this will enable you to work smarter, not harder. You will be in a stronger position to grow forward as a strong and healthy, effective and successful congregation in mission.

As your congregation develops a helpful long-range plan, you can nurture forward the group's best compassion, wisdom, judgment, vision, common sense, and prayer. You can pool together these major qualities to discover the best direction for your congregation—to discover the few key objectives, the 20 percenters that will deliver 80 percent of the future.

I have seen congregations make the mistake of developing thick, ninety-seven-page long-range planning documents. They gather every idea tentatively proposed for probable consideration and discussion. This is what I affectionately call the "cafeteria list" approach to long-range planning. The document accomplishes two excellent things. First, it sits on a shelf that would otherwise be empty and lonely. Second, it gathers dust that would otherwise have to be gathered in some other part of the galaxies.

The best long-range plans are short—one to three pages long. Occasionally, four to five pages long. These plans identify and include only the 20 percenters that will deliver 80 percent of the future for the congregation. To be sure, we will do the 80 percenters each year as they come to us. We will do them with faithfulness and integrity. And they will deliver 20 percent of the results. But none of the 80 percenters are included in our plan. We include only the 20 percenters that will deliver 80 percent of the results.

This is why developing an effective long-range plan is an art. As leaders, you know your congregation and community best. You have studied the *Twelve Keys,* the central characteristics, of healthy, effective congregations. The art is to pool, to mutually share, the qualities that will help you grow forward a healthy future.

Compassion

Compassion is sharing, caring, giving, loving, and serving. The spirit of compassion leads us to the key 20 percenters that yield 80 percent of the results, accomplishments, and achievements. Compassion is generous and grace-filled. Compassion helps us to live beyond ourselves.

Some congregations have become too "caught up in themselves." They have an egocentric view of life. They focus only on what "works for them." They are interested in what will help them survive or in what will help them grow. Either is a preoccupation with the congregation.

People are not drawn to a congregation whose message is: "Come, join us so we will survive." People are not drawn to a congregation whose message is: "Come, join us so we can grow." Neither surviving nor getting bigger is compelling.

People are drawn to a congregation where they can both receive and give compassion. They are not looking only to receive compassion. They are looking for a grouping where they can share their compassion in a worthwhile cause. At heart, people have a generous gift of compassion.

When we find someone who is selfish and stingy, we have not found someone who is selfish and stingy. We have found someone who is scared or scarred, or both. They are using "stingy and selfish" as self-protective mechanisms so as to not be scared or scarred yet another time.

Compassion is rich and generous, gentle and thoughtful. Compassion is not syrupy or sentimental. It is not co-dependent and dependent. It is not gushy and gooey. It does not reek of weepy, maudlin sentimentality. Our gift of compassion helps us to live beyond ourselves.

Some objectives will stir your deepest compassion. Your compassion is teaching you that these objectives are key 20 percenter objectives. Do these. As these objectives have stirred your compassion, they will stir the compassion of others. You will have good company as, together, you achieve these 20 percenters.

Wisdom

I once observed that the primary difference between the two words *no* and *now* is the *w* for *wisdom*. Wisdom is the capacity to see the strengths people have for living a whole, healthy life in the grace of God. Wisdom is the capacity to discern, understand, and appreciate the dynamics operating in a given group of persons.

Wisdom is the capacity to discern the ways in which the motivation of compassion, community, hope, challenge, reasonability, and commitment encourage a group to move forward. Wisdom is the capacity to value the dynamics of memory, change, conflict, and hope, and how these are distinctively affecting and shaping each "now" event, each "now" in the life of a congregation.

It takes considerable wisdom to discern the ways in which these influences live themselves out in the particular sociological, economic, cultural, vocational, and theological patterns present in a specific local congregation. It takes wisdom to think through ways one can best help in the light of the key characteristics of a given local congregation and community.

Judgment

You are invited to evaluate and develop a realistic assessment of your congregation's present strengths and possibilities. You are encouraged to choose the primary direction for your future. You are invited to discover your maximum mission potential. You are invited to decide the range of persons your congregation plans to serve in mission each year. You are encouraged to claim your congregation's strengths. You are invited to expand a current strength and add a new strength.

The art is to exercise judgment. We form a wise, thoughtful estimation. We discern and compare. We accurately assess and evaluate where our congregation stands in relation to each of the **Twelve Keys.** It does not help to overestimate or to underestimate. Judgment is the capacity to see where you really are.

This invites you to put aside generalizations of where you hope you could be, to put aside sentimental notions of where you wish you could be, and to put aside doom-and-gloom thoughts of how bad you think it might be. You are invited to bring to bear your best judgment to achieve an accurate, thoughtful diagnosis of your realistic strengths and weaknesses. This invites your best mutual judgment.

Vision

Long-range planning invites our best vision . . . . our powerful imagination, thoughtful discernment, and creative foresight. We need vision that is responsible and realistic, not naive and idealistic . . . . vision that is courageous and compassionate, not timid and calculating . . . . vision that is prayerful and powerful, not self-centered and weak.

In developing your plan, you compare, think through, and select the few key objectives that will best expand or add specific strengths in your local congregation. This invites considerable vision. We see beyond what has been. We see what can be. We see what will be.

One of the helpful, decisive watershed questions in life and in long-range planning is, "Do you believe your best years are before you or behind you?" I have known people in their late eighties, dim of eyesight, hard of hearing, limping on a cane, who are convinced that with God's grace some of their best years are before them. I have also known people in their early twenties who, sadly, have convinced themselves that their best years are behind them.

It is a self-fulfilling prophecy. Those people and those congregations convinced that their best years are behind them will not be disappointed. Those congregations that look back to the glory years of the church culture of the 1950s, when their sanctuaries were filled to the brim, have already become has-been congregations.

Those people and those congregations that are convinced and confident that some of their best years in mission are before them will not be disappointed. The prophecy fulfills itself. Those congregations that look forward to the future in mission that God has both promised and prepared for them will not be disappointed. Some of their best years are before them. This invites our best vision.

Common Sense

Sometimes, one of the best things a consultant shares with a local congregation is common sense. Sometimes, one of the best things we share with one another is our common sense as to what will work, what can work, what won't work, and what can't work. Common sense is the capacity to claim the things that are working and to fix some things that are broken. We recognize that "when it's working, we don't fix it." We recognize that "if it's not broken, we don't fix it." Common sense is down-to-earth.

A congregation that has realistic, commonsense objectives will avoid the dilemma of procrastination. Pure procrastination is not often found in congregations. But people do sometimes postpone or put off taking action on objectives. The cause can be traced to their compulsiveness toward perfectionism.

Some congregations set objectives that are too many, set too high, to be accomplished too soon. Some set objectives that are unrealistic, grandiose, and glittering with generalities. People see, intuitively and innately, that the objectives cannot be achieved. Most people prefer to succeed, not fail.

Thus, people postpone action to postpone failure. They put off action when faced with too many objectives, set too high. They innately sense they will fall short. They sense they have set themselves up to fail. They sense they are doomed to failure.

The real dilemma is a compulsiveness toward perfectionism. The solution is common sense. Set a few key objectives that are realistic and achievable, have solid time horizons, and match with our strengths. Whenever a group has objectives so grandiose they cannot be achieved, people procrastinate and postpone action. They mentally kick themselves for procrastinating. They would be better off kicking themselves for their compulsiveness toward perfectionism. One of the things that counters this compulsiveness is common sense, making it one of the best qualities for developing an effective long-range plan.

Prayer

One of the best things Christians do is pray together. When we seek to discern those 20 percenters that will deliver 80 percent of the future, the best thing we can do is to pray to God for the compassion, wisdom, judgment, vision, and common sense God can grant us.

It is amazing to me how many congregations, when they do long-range planning, act more like amateur sociologists than called-of-God Christians. They never pray. They study reams upon reams of data, as though the more data they study, the more the data will tell them what to do. The truth of the matter is that the more data they study, the more confused they become. The data themselves do not tell the direction forward.

One of the best things Christians do together is pray. And one of the best things we can do in developing an effective long-range plan is to pray. In Jeremiah 29:11 (RSV) we discover God's words to the prophet Jeremiah: "For I know the plans I have for you . . . plans for welfare and not for evil, to give you a future and a hope."

Let God have a say in God's congregation.

Our real hope is to seek the future that God has both promised and is preparing for your congregation, not fabricating the future we want. We are seeking to have sufficient compassion, wisdom, judgment, vision, and common sense to discern and to discover the ways in which God is inviting this congregation to be in mission in its long-range future.

Planning invites our best prayer.

The spirit of our long-range planning conversations can include an attitude of thoughtful, reverent prayer. It is helpful to invite some group in the congregation to pray on behalf of and for all the participants developing your congregation's plan.

Pray that God's rich, full grace will be manifest in your sharing together so the mission of your congregation will be blessed and enriched.

Planning and prayer go together. Congregations with a strong track record of action, implementation, and momentum have developed a prayer life that has about it the qualities of compassion, wisdom, judgment, vision, and common sense.

The invitational questions shared at the beginning of this chapter will help to focus your congregation's prayer life. In helping your congregation to focus its prayer life for planning, your congregation can hold before itself these invitational questions:

Where are we headed?
What kind of future are we building?
What are our strengths, gifts, and competencies?
Who is God inviting us to serve in mission?

These invitational questions are particularly appropriate focal points for the prayer life of your congregation as it shares in developing an effective long-range plan.

You are not praying for precise, definitive, once-for-all-time answers to these invitational questions. Rather, the spirit of your prayer life together is rooted in asking for God's grace and guidance as you pray and puzzle through where you are headed, the kind of future you are building, the strengths, gifts and competencies you have, and the mission you plan to serve.

Frequently, these invitational questions are shared richly and fully with the congregation. Much is at stake in the development of an effective long-range plan. Since much is at stake, we are called to pray with the compassion, wisdom, judgment, vision, and common sense that come to us as gifts from God.

Whom We Pray For. Invite the whole congregation to share in prayer on behalf of all the persons who are helping to develop your plan. Pray with and for the key leaders facilitating the development of the congregation's long-range plan. Encourage all persons to pray that their own excellent ideas, good suggestions, thoughtful judgments, and realistic visions will contribute creatively and constructively to fashioning the future for the congregation.

Further, encourage the congregation to pray for the pastor and the staff so that their shepherding, caring, insights, compassion, and competencies will be particularly present in "this time." Finally, encourage the congregation to pray for all of the people this congregation now serves and the persons the congregation hopes to serve in mission.

In response to the question, "Who is my neighbor?" Jesus told the parable of the Good Samaritan. One helpful understanding of the parable is that the neighbor is the man, beaten and robbed, in the ditch. This interpretation affirms that the good neighbor is the one who calls forth the best in the other. The man in the ditch called forth the best in the Samaritan who, in the centuries come and gone, has been called the Good Samaritan.

Mission is mutual. The person we are helping is helping us to live our lives at our serving best. When we seek to help with specific human hurts and hopes, it is a mutual process. Sometimes, it is finally hard to determine who is helping whom the most. It is important that our prayer life, during this time of planning and expectancy, includes looking forward to helping and to being helped by people whom we have not yet had the privilege of meeting.

Praying Without Ceasing. We begin and conclude each planning conversation with prayer—prayer that is not full of abstract generalities and vague, ambiguous concerns. But each time of prayer can richly and deeply invite the full, stirring presence of God, who dwells with us and among us as we plan in the midst of the grace of God.

You can invite the whole congregation to be in an attitude, spirit, and time of prayer during the weeks in which the long-range plan is being developed. Further, it is helpful to invite a specific group of people to have the privilege of praying for your work together as you seek to discover and discern the future in mission that God has both promised and prepared for your congregation.

I recall a congregation in which a vibrant, caring, men's prayer breakfast group took upon itself the rich, full task, as the congregation engaged in developing its plan, of praying for the congregation, for the key leaders, for the pastor, for the staff, and for the countless people the congregation would serve in the years to come.

I recall another congregation where it was the Wednesday night Bible study group that shared this task and privilege. In yet another congregation it was one of the women's circles that contributed to the prayer life of the planning venture. It is important that some group be invited to carry forward this sense of prayer in the midst of planning.

The practice of praying can be a standard way of life in a local congregation. When we invite leaders to achieve a key objective, we pray for or with them during the time they are achieving the key objective. In many congregations, there is a time of praying with and for the Sunday School teachers before their classes, a time of praying with and for the chairpersons and the committees substantively engaged in the administrative and decision-making life of the congregation, and a time of praying with and for the mission teams, the visitation teams, the choir, the significant relational groups—all those people and groupings that share in serving in the life and mission of the congregation.

CHRIST AT THE DOOR

We discover possibilities for our future with the four invitational questions. We discover possibilities for our future as we live the qualities of compassion, wisdom, judgment, vision, common sense, and prayer. We discover possibilities for our future as we discover Christ's invitation with us.

I was helping one congregation. We were in their sanctuary, praying and puzzling for the future of their congregation. One of the best things we do as Christians is pray. They had had thirty-seven losing seasons. We needed to gather all the prayer we could.

In the center wall of the chancel they have a remarkable stained glass window of Christ standing at the door, knocking. You remember the picture, the window, the Biblical image. In the long lost churched culture of an earlier time, the under-standing of the picture, the window, the Biblical image was, "Christ stands at the door, knocking, hoping someone will hear the knock, and come to the door, and open the door and invite Christ **in** to their lives."

And, much was made of the fact that there was no doorknob or latchstring or keyhole on the outside of the door. We would be the ones who would hear the knock, and we would come to the door, and we would open the door, and we would invite Christ **in** to our lives.

It dawned on me that day as we were kneeling at the altar rail, praying, with the sunlight streaming through the stained glass window in a remarkable kind of way, what the picture, the window, the Biblical image means in our time, "Christ stands at the door, knocking, hoping someone will hear the knock, and come to the door, and open the door so Christ can invite them **out** into his life in mission."

Good friends, it is no longer that we invite Christ **in** to our lives. Now, Christ invites us **out into His life.** Where is Christ? In mission. Where does Christ live and die and is risen again and again? Among the human hurts and hopes God has planted all around us. Christ is in the world. When we are in the world, we are with Christ. It is not that we discover Christ, then go and serve in mission. It is in the sharing of mission that we discover Christ. In this new day, Christ invites us **out** . . . . to live and serve with him in mission.

8

WHAT TO LISTEN FOR AND LOOK FOR

WHAT TO LISTEN FOR

As you develop your long-range plan, you will generate considerable creativity.

Many participants will share excellent ideas and good suggestions. They will share their best wisdom as to the congregation's strengths, competencies, and gifts. They may share some of the congregation's problems, weaknesses, and shortcomings. The *Twelve Keys* planning process is designed to facilitate a rich, full sharing of these materials. Considerable analysis, diagnosis, and possibilities will emerge.

In developing your long-range plan, it is important that you, other key leaders, your pastor, and all participants have some sense of what to listen for. You will discover many excellent ideas and good suggestions, much analysis and diagnosis. In the midst of this multitude of information and possibilities, I encourage you to listen at three levels.

First, listen *for what is said.* Listen with considerable thought and care to precisely what is being said. People have an extraordinary ability to teach you where they are at and what they think. They do so by what they say.

In one congregation, a woman raised her hand during the third stage of the process and said, "Dr. Callahan, what we need is a larger choir." Some of the people in the room, who sat near the back of the sanctuary on that Sunday morning, thought she was saying, "What we need is a louder choir." They themselves had trouble hearing the choir when they sat underneath the overhang of the balcony. The choir director thought she was saying, "What we need is a choir that sings more classical music so that it will be considered among the finer choirs in the city." He thought he was reading between the lines but missed the call on both counts.

What she actually said was, "We need a larger choir." What she precisely meant was that theirs was a choir of twenty, and she felt it was important that there be at least thirty people in the choir, given the size of the sanctuary and the ways in which a choir of thirty would contribute to the sense of stirring and inspiring worship.

Frequently, leaders confuse what they think was said for what was actually said. Or, they listen for what they think should have been said. Both of these are grievous mistakes and can finally confuse the development of an effective long-range plan. Listen for what is really said.

Second, listen *between the lines.* People sometimes make statements, tentatively fishing to see if their idea is acceptable or if others will hear between the lines and pick up on what they really want to say. They may feel freer to express what they want to say if one of the leaders indicates that he or she understands what they are trying to say and then restates it more fully.

In one congregation I served as a consultant, the church secretary said, "Sometimes, Dr. Callahan, I think I have been here long enough." In the fuller conversation that followed I discovered that she was really tired of the stressful relationship that had emerged between her and the choir director. In her initial statement, she was tentatively fishing to discover whether she could more fully share her own concerns.

Third, listen *for what is not said.* As a consultant, I learn as much from what is not said as from the other two guidelines put together. When I am working with a congregation and we are analyzing stirring, helpful worship, the fact that nothing is said about the preaching tells me a lot. If nothing is said about the preaching, one can conclude that people think reasonably well of this pastor, see his or her strengths in a variety of ways, and understand that, at least for the moment, preaching is not one of them.

If a group is analyzing pastoral and lay visitation in the community and a good deal is said about the pastor's shepherding and the ways in which he or she is helpful in visitation, one learns a great deal by what is not said about the visitation done by key leaders in that congregation.

These guidelines for listening illustrate the best way to learn about the strengths, competencies, shortcomings, and weaknesses of your congregation.

WHAT TO LOOK FOR

First, look for *the strengths you already have well in place.* The ***Twelve Keys*** chart encourages people to look, in holistic, integrative, dynamic ways, at the whole of the twelve characteristics at one time. No one characteristic stands alone; each relates to some of the other characteristics on the chart.

People make two mistakes when they look at the chart. First, they become too concerned about whether their congregation has all twelve. Well, it would be fun and helpful if, on our football team, we had a first string of all-pro players. As a matter of fact, the team will be a winning team with nine pro players. Likewise, congregations are strong and healthy, effective and successful with nine out of the twelve central characteristics well in place as foundational strengths.

The second mistake people make is to look at the chart and focus on what the congregation lacks. If you look first for what you do not have, you will tend to miss seeing what you do have. At the first practice of the season, the wise coach looks over the players who have come out for practice and asks, "What do we have going for us this year? Is this the year of power, blocking, and a running game, or is this the year of speed, quickness, and a passing game?" The wise congregation looks first for what it has going for it: its strengths, gifts, and competencies.

Second, look for *the effects of transitions,* of changeovers, in pastoral and key leadership positions. The more rapid the transitions, the more leadership discontinuity in the congregation, and the tougher it is to develop momentum. Wherever there is an excellent match between a pastor and a congregation, the most productive years in that relationship *begin* in the fifth, sixth, and seventh years.

One congregation I helped had had an excellent match between pastor and people from 1920 to 1931. That foundational eleven-year period provided the strength out of which that congregation has faced the twists and turns of life's vicissitudes in the following years. Frequently, wherever one has a solid, strong congregation, one can look back to a time when there was an excellent match well in place for five, six, seven, or more years.

Consider the transitions in leadership that have affected the momentum and dynamic of your congregation. I know of a congregation that has been in existence for ninety-three years and has had thirty-seven pastors. One can imagine the transitions of leadership that occurred in that congregation. Discontinuity, disruptiveness, competitiveness, and a climate of lack of trust contribute considerably to and result from a high turnover in both the pastoral and key leadership of a congregation. It is important to think through how one might bring about and keep in place the rich, full benefits of a good match between key leaders, pastor, and people.

Third, look for *those strong, hope-fulfilling events* that inform this congregation's life and sense of future. In the case of one congregation, way back in 1917 some of their deepest longings, yearnings, and hopes were dramatically fulfilled in a decisive event. In 1917, 1918, 1919, and every year since then they have celebrated that event in which some of their deepest longings and hopes were decisively fulfilled. Look for the hope-fulfilling events that inform a congregation's life and give it a sense of identity, continuity, and fulfilled hope as it looks to the future.

Fourth, look for *and understand those traumatic events* that have marred and scarred a congregation's life together. In one congregation during one year, four couples—some of the congregation's leaders—went through the pain and disruption of separation. Some individuals were involved with other people. There were four divorces and, finally, three remarriages. That year was one of the most traumatic, bizarre, difficult years in the life of that congregation.

People are still building forward their life together as a congregation, silently hoping that nothing like that is going to happen again. The scar is twenty years old, and it seems to be well healed, but it cannot be erased completely. In another congregation, an excellent choir director, for whatever reasons, moved abruptly to another part of the country. The move and the trauma of that beloved choir director's rapid departure has meant that certain things no longer happen in the congregation in the rich, full ways in which they used to.

Finally, look and listen for *the influences of everyday, ordinary life.* Sometimes, we put on "congregation glasses" and only view those programs and activities that are directly a part of a congregation's life. As a matter of fact, hope-fulfilling events and traumatic events that occur in the everyday lives of people in a congregation decisively affect and shape what is going on in that congregation.

Frequently, these events occur among the informal relational neighborhood networks of a congregation. People in our time live in many neighborhoods. They do not primarily live in a geographical neighborhood. Regrettably, more often than not congregations tend to focus on the geographical neighborhood.

I encourage you to "see" these neighborhoods. People live mostly in these neighborhoods:

Informal relational and friendship neighborhoods
Vocational village neighborhoods
Common interests neighborhoods
Life stages neighborhoods

Human hurts and hopes neighborhoods
Recreational neighborhoods
Music and arts neighborhoods

Listen for and look for what is taking place, has recently taken place, and will likely be taking place in these neighborhood networks that are strongly a part of the life and work of this congregation.

You will accomplish a helpful long-range plan by deepening your alertness and sensitivity to what to listen for and what to look for. You will come to a better self-understanding of who you are and of who you will be. This will immeasurably advance the strength and health of the future you develop.

9

PRINCIPLES FOR PARTICIPATION

Many congregations use these six principles for participation to increase the sharing, involvement, and contributions of the whole congregation. The more persons who are aware of these participation principles, the more constructive your congregation's planning and sense of direction. When you maximize participation in creating your future plan, you create a rich, more helpful plan and strong ownership for achieving the plan.

The six principles for participation are:

Encourage looking at the whole
Develop a long-range view
Encourage a processive, dynamic view
Share your wisdom
Use "Yes" voting
Create a planning team

The more fully these six principles are followed, the more likely your congregation is to develop an effective long-range plan for its future . . . . and the deeper the ownership for the plan.

PRINCIPLE 1. ENCOURAGE LOOKING AT THE WHOLE

Encourage looking at the whole. You will increase participation. You can help every person who participates in your congregation's long-range planning to look at the whole—to have a holistic, integrative perspective, not a segmented and departmental view. Encourage each person to serve as a "representative" of the whole, not a representative of the parts.

Sometimes, people are active in one department of a congregation's life. They love that department. They invest their time in that department. It may be the children's department, the music department, the youth department, and so on. Some of them have a tendency to see the congregation only through that department.

As you look at the *Twelve Keys* chart, you will see the chart invites everyone to look at your congregation as a whole. We look at the twelve central characteristics of a healthy, effective congregation with a holistic, integrative, dynamic perspective rather than a segmentalist, departmental, compartmentalized perspective. Each participant is encouraged to nurture this capacity to see the whole.

In developing a long-range plan, some people make a serious mistake. They bring together people who are leaders or advocates of various segments and departments within the congregation. Then, they ask them to try to look at the whole. It is sometimes difficult for a leader or an advocate of some specific segment or department to focus on the whole. Indeed, some persons are caught up in their department, loving their department, and giving leadership in their department of the congregation's work. They have a tendency to continue to focus on their department.

We encourage everyone to look at the whole, not the parts.

When a long-range planning group consists only of representatives of various departments, they will tend to find themselves in the old dilemma of being unable to see the forest for the trees. Everybody got to the planning gathering because he or she is representing some "tree." Each advocate brings his or her own tree to the table, intending to assure that it receives its fair share of water. The group develops a good give and take. Everyone cooperates genuinely in coordinating a plan that gives each tree its fair share of water.

But the group is preoccupied with representing each specific department and protecting individual "turf" in the long-range plan. In this setting, people have difficulty seeing the whole forest they might be able to grow forward. For long-range planning, it is not helpful to select only people who have a vested interest in a specific department of the congregation's work.

Further, a planning group that gathered primarily to "represent" the parts tends to see only the parts gathered around the table. They tend to not see any possibilities that are not already represented. They miss new possibilities that open the future more fully for the congregation.

In **Twelve Keys** *planning, people get to the planning sessions because they are part of the congregation, not because they represent a part of the congregation.*

We encourage grassroots persons to participate in the planning. We encourage persons who share in some grouping to participate. We encourage informal and formal leaders, pastor, and staff to participate. They are not there because they represent a part. All of them come, representing the congregation as a whole.

We encourage people to see the whole.

PRINCIPLE 2. DEVELOP A LONG-RANGE FOCUS

Encourage a long-range focus. You will increase participation. Many people, given half a chance, have the capacity to look long-range. Some of the most helpful persons in developing an effective plan are those persons who can look ahead . . . . who are able to perceive a long-range time horizon rather than an annual time horizon.

Generally, many of these persons are in the grassroots of a congregation. It is precisely these persons who are important to include in developing your long-range plan. They are not caught up in a specific departmental *annual* leadership task and, therefore, have a capacity to look at the whole in long-range ways.

Encourage all persons who participate to have a long-range focus . . . . to have the capacity to look three, five, seven, and ten years ahead. Encourage people who, in their day-to-day work and life, develop future plans and consider the long-range view of things. Most people, with encouragement, have the experience and skills to look ahead to long-range time horizons. Many people, given half a chance, can distinguish the long-range, important priorities from the short-term, urgent issues.

There is a difference between *important* and *urgent*. Some objectives are important and urgent. Some are important, not urgent. Important objectives, whether urgent or not, have significant worth and consequence. They are 20 percenter objectives. Over the long term, these will deliver the future. Encourage people to look in long-range ways at both the important and urgent and the important, not the urgent, objectives.

Some objectives are urgent, not important. They clamor for immediate attention.

Some persons have a tendency to focus on urgent, but not important issues. They do this because they are looking for activities that deliver quick closure, short-term, immediate-satisfaction results. In long-range planning we do not allow ourselves to get sidetracked by "urgent, not important" and "not important, not urgent" matters. Encourage people to focus on important, long-range possibilities.

We develop an effective long-range plan in order to know what makes best sense to achieve today. The purpose of long-range planning is so a congregation can be where it wants to be in the coming years. We decide where we want to be in the long run precisely so we will know what makes sense to achieve today and tomorrow.

We set the date for the wedding. Then, we work backwards. Once we know the date for the wedding, we know when the rehearsal dinner is, when the showers happen, when the gown is selected, when the invitations are sent out, and so on. We do not work from today forward. We work from the wedding date backward.

This long-range focus develops an effective plan for your congregation. Look to where you want to be so you will know what makes sense to do now.

PRINCIPLE 3. ENCOURAGE A SWIFT, PROCESSIVE, DYNAMIC VIEW

Encourage a swift, processive, dynamic view. You will increase participation. Encourage every participant to develop a swift, processive, dynamic perspective of long-range planning, not a slow, rigid, block view. Effective long-range planning is ongoing and productive, focused on the end results.

An old way of doing long-range planning was to choose a specific time horizon, such as three years, and develop a long-range plan for that block of time. It isolated smaller blocks of time as year 1, year 2, and year 3. It steadfastly moved sequentially through each of the blocks for all three years of the plan, looking neither right nor left to evaluate, revise, change, or improve.

The slow, rigid, block approach had two difficulties. One, it tended to defer new possibilities to the next three-year cycle. The message tended to be, "That is an excellent idea. Be sure to bring it up when we get to our next three-year plan." The benefits of an excellent new possibility are deferred to another time, and, sometimes, lost and forgotten.

Two, the slow, rigid, block approach tended to create a "front load" phenomenon. People tended to put too many objectives, set too high, to be accomplished too soon *in the first year* of a three-year static plan. Intuitively, they sensed that they would not get the chance to add to the plan for three years.

In their enthusiasm, they tried to do too much too soon. Then, they postponed action to postpone failure.

That slow, rigid, block understanding is less helpful in our time.

The better way forward is for your congregation to select whatever time horizon makes best sense to you—three, five, seven, or ten years. Then, you can develop a swift, processive, dynamic approach to your long-range planning.

For example, the best time horizon for a specific local congregation might be three years. In the current year, we decide the keys to expand and to add, along with specific key objectives related to each of these keys. We set timelines for the coming three years.

In the swift, processive, dynamic approach, toward the end of the first year, we achieve two steps.

1. We advance the plan for the remaining two years. We delete some objectives. We modify some objectives. We include a new objective that has recently come to us. In effect, we create a new year 1 and a new year 2.
2. Then, we add the new third year. We include key objectives that build on the ones we are achieving and that help us to be a strong, healthy congregation. We are always looking three years ahead.

This approach has considerable merit over the old slow, rigid, block approach:

1. We pace ourselves. We do not "front load" the first year.
2. We are open to new possibilities now. We give people the confidence that their new, excellent ideas and good suggestions will be considered now.
3. We give ourselves the ability to evaluate, modify, improve, and advance our key objectives each year.
4. We give ourselves the ability to add key objectives and timelines for the new next year in ways that contribute to the rhythm of momentum and dynamic we are developing.

Thus, we encourage persons to think in swift, processive, dynamic ways.

PRINCIPLE 4. SHARE YOUR WISDOM

Encourage persons to share their wisdom. You will increase participation. Help every person have the confidence and assurance that they have wisdom. Help them to share their excellent ideas and good suggestions. People, given half a chance, have wisdom. What takes wisdom is fostering and developing the distinctive, unique strengths of your congregation, not conforming to conventional notions of what a church should be.

For example, some congregations become preoccupied with demographics. Some become involved in what I call the "demographic captivity" of the church. Historically, there was the Babylonian captivity of the people of Israel. In the 1950s, there emerged the "suburban captivity" of the congregation. The myth emerged that to be effective and successful as a congregation, one had to look like a busy, bustling, successful, suburban congregation of the 1950s.

Regrettably, rural congregations, inner-city congregations, village congregations, county seat congregations, large downtown congregations, neighborhood congregations, and regional congregations tried to follow suit. They became preoccupied with trying to mimic the busy, bustling suburban congregations of that time. They stopped doing what they did best. To this day, some people assume that when we start a new congregation, it is best to create a busy, bustling suburban congregation of the 1950s.

The Christian faith survived, thrived, and moved forward in its mission for more than one thousand and nine hundred plus years without ever knowing what a busy, bustling suburban congregation, a la the 1950s, looked like. Fortunately, we have almost grown beyond the suburban captivity of the church. Yet, we are still involved in the demographic captivity of the church.

There is no *direct* correlation between population growth and church growth.

All over the planet, congregations are weak and declining or dying amidst growing populations. They are not delivering nine out of the twelve central characteristics. The earlier assumption of the church culture was correct. When the population grew, congregations grew. When the population declined, congregations declined. This was true because much of the population was a church culture.

We live in a mission culture. All over the planet, congregations are strong and healthy because they are delivering nine out of the twelve central characteristics of an effective congregation. Even when the population in a county or township has declined over the past twenty years, the percentage of the total population that is effectively unchurched has usually increased. Congregations are strong and healthy because they are reaching their fair share of the increased unchurched population in the county or township.

When I am in the southeast, church members there tell me if it weren't for all of the Southern Baptists, they would be doing better. When I am on the West Coast, people there tell me if it weren't for all the nondenominational congregations, they would be doing better.

When I am in the northeast, church members there tell me if it weren't for all of the Roman Catholics, they would be doing better. Some time ago, while helping a congregation near Boston, I visited with a Roman Catholic priest. He said to me, "You know, Dr. Callahan, if it weren't for all the Congregationalists, we'd be doing better."

It's almost as if the phrase is "If it weren't for all the *(fill in the blank),* we'd be doing better." The truth of the matter is: the largest "denomination" in the country is the denomination of the unchurched. The truth of the matter is: the demographics have some bearing, but not a decisive, final bearing.

Can you imagine Paul on the dock at Corinth, watching the sail of the ship on the horizon, eagerly and expectantly waiting there at the dock for that ship to bring to him the latest demographic printouts from the computer in Rome so he would know where to go next to witness to the Gospel?

I do want to affirm that demographic study has its important place. For years, I have taken into consideration the demographic data of countless communities across this planet. At the same time, it is most important that the demographic data not enslave us to a future that someone else has projected.

You can focus your mutual compassion, wisdom, judgment, vision, common sense, and prayer on the future God has both promised and is preparing for your congregation in mission. You can encourage participants to have the quality and spirit of wisdom about their lives and their congregation.

PRINCIPLE 5. USE "YES" VOTING

Encourage persons to share in "Yes" voting. You will increase participation. The principle of "Yes" voting helps to limit the amount of time spent planning. We focus our conversations on our 20 percenters. We select our key expands and adds and the key objectives for each with "Yes" voting. These become the major priorities of the congregation.

In the chapter on Celebration Planning, Chapter Twelve, I share the steps in how to do "Yes" voting. Here, I want to confirm that the two-person teams, the small groups, the sharing in the whole group, and the "Yes" voting process have, again and again, been helpful with countless congregations across the planet.

The principle of "Yes" voting assures everyone that they will have a voice in developing the future. Someone develops an excellent idea.

1. They reflect on their idea and improve it.
2. They share it with their team partner. The idea is advanced.
3. The two-person team shares the idea with two other teams. The idea is further improved.

4. The idea is shared with the whole gathering. It is further advanced.

People have confidence and ownership for moving the idea forward.

Because we have several small groups, we will usually have several possibilities under consideration. "Yes" voting encourages a positive, affirmative method of selecting the optimum choices. In "Yes" voting, each team and small group is given multiple choices. Each team is given the number of choices equal to half of the total number of possibilities under consideration, plus one more.

If eight possibilities are being considered, each team and small group is given four choices, plus one more, for a total of five choices. If twelve possibilities are being considered, each group is given six choices, plus one more—for a total of seven choices.

When the choices are tabulated, several possibilities usually have a solid consensus.

Do not turn "Yes" voting into "no" voting. Someone may suggest that time would be saved if, in an original voting on ten possibilities, every team had four "no" votes rather than six "Yes" votes. Under that suggestion, each team would vote against the four they did not want. Do not do that. The time saved will not make up for the momentum lost. It is far more constructive and creative for the congregation to be voting in favor of what they are for rather than voting for what they would be against.

The principle of "Yes" voting is helpful in advancing the constructive, creative character of your planning sessions. It is an excellent principle to use whenever a group is considering multiple possibilities. In straightforward, constructive ways, it helps the congregation discover the consensus of its best way forward.

PRINCIPLE 6. CREATE A PLANNING TEAM

Encourage creating a planning team. You will increase participation. Invite five to eight to twelve persons to serve as your planning team. This team will help your congregation move forward with the steps of

Creative Study
Celebration Planning
Act Swiftly

These steps are discussed in Part Three. For now, it is helpful to confirm that some of the team may give leadership to the Creative Study step, some to the Celebration Planning step, and some to the Act Swiftly step.

This planning team helps the congregation create its plan.

This team does not create the plan. The planning team helps the congregation move through the steps to create a strong, healthy future. We limit the size of the planning team to just enough people that the team will concentrate primarily on helping the grassroots and key leaders of your whole congregation develop a helpful long-range plan.

A planning team that is too large tends to turn itself into "a junior congregation planning committee." The larger group ends up trying to develop the plan by itself. They, then, have an ownership problem. They have ownership for "their" plan. The congregation does not. They now have to try and "sell" their plan to the congregation.

The *Twelve Keys* planning process is a *congregational* way. Everyone in the congregation is encouraged to participate in the Study, Plan, and Act Swiftly steps.

It is not a "representative" process where persons who have "functional leadership posts" gather to represent the congregation as a whole. In the *Twelve Keys* approach, every person in the congregation is encouraged to represent themselves. All are welcome to help shape the congregations' future.

By whatever name you call the planning team, their task is to facilitate the widest participation possible from among the congregation in developing an effective long-range plan. It is not the purpose of this group to decide the long-range plan.

The focus of the planning team is to give leadership as the congregation develops an effective long-range plan.

The planning team serves as major resource people with the congregation. They are the "resident resource persons" on the principles and materials in:

Twelve Keys to an Effective Church, Second Edition
The Twelve Keys Leaders' Guide
The Twelve Keys Bible Study

Frequently, the planning team discovers which two or three persons on the team would have fun being the primary "resident resource persons" on each of the three books.

The planning team gives leadership to helping the congregation to study, plan, and act swiftly. People participate when they know the planning team is there to help the whole congregation create the plan for our future.

Your congregation can practice the principles for participation:

Encourage looking at the whole
Develop a long-range view
Encourage a processive, dynamic view
Share your wisdom
Use "Yes" voting
Create a planning team

You will be blessed with a strong, healthy future.

Part Three

DEVELOPING YOUR CONGREGATION

10

PLANNING AND ACTION

PURPOSE

The purpose of planning is action, not planning.

More fully, the purpose of planning is action, achievements, and accomplishments. Purposeful action results in achievements and accomplishments. There is no merit in action for the sake of action. When we head in the wrong direction with considerable action, we simply achieve the wrong destination quicker and faster.

The purpose of planning is to discover a strong, healthy direction . . . . to head toward constructive action that results in achievements and accomplishments. The purpose of planning is mission, not meetings. The purpose of planning is accomplishments and achievements, not more activities and longer planning reports.

Merrill Douglass, leading time management consultant and a good friend, has created what is called Douglass's Law of Clutter: "Clutter expands to fill the space available." A person may have a desk, with lots of stacks and stacks, piles and clutter . . . . a mess. The thought comes, "If only I had a second desk." Now, the person has two desks, with lots of stacks and stacks, piles and clutter . . . . a mess.

Callahan's Law of Planning is: "Planning expands to fill the time available . . . . therefore, limit the amount of time for planning."

Many congregations make the mistake of assuming that long-range planning should take a long time. Some congregations have had long-range planning committees that have been in existence for several years. They have yet to develop a single long-range objective. They almost work out of the assumption that the longer they take, the better the plan. Not true. The more straightforward and streamlined the work of the congregation and the planning team, the better the long-range plan.

Limit the amount of time you are willing to invest in planning. As a result, you will be more likely to center on the 20 percenters. The more time people allow for planning, the more they succumb to a preoccupation with details, leading to analysis paralysis. The more time people allow for planning, the more they dawdle with objectives that are really 80 percenters and that detract from rich, full discussion of those few 20 percenters that will best advance the future of their congregation.

Regrettably, some people assume that the more time they spend in planning, the more commitment they are demonstrating. They are simply demonstrating that they do **not** know how to plan well. Encourage people to limit the amount of time they invest in planning.

The purpose of **The Twelve Keys Leaders' Guide** is to help your congregation move toward action, accomplishment, and achievement, not more planning, more meetings, and longer reports. This book is designed to provide you with the resources to help your congregation develop its future in a timely, straightforward, streamlined way.

The Leaders' Guide is a companion book to **Twelve Keys to an Effective Church, Second Edition**. This is the foundational, classic text to help your congregation discover, develop, and decide its future. **The Twelve Keys Bible Study** is a helpful companion resource. Together, these three works form a trilogy of planning resources for your congregation. Together, these resources will help you develop a strong, healthy congregation.

The art is to invest almost enough time in planning so we head to the action. A streamlined plan creates streamlined action. We move forward.

SOMETHING WILL WORK

In considering the nature of long-range planning, compare these three logical options:

1. Something will work.
2. Nothing will work.
3. Everything will work.

It is not realistic to believe that everything will work. Of the three options, the third can be immediately disregarded. Only someone with an excessive compulsive addictive perfectionism would assume that everything will work. Some things will not work. Some things will be excellent mistakes. Feel free to *not* work out of the conviction that everything will work.

It is even more important that you *not* work out of the conviction that nothing will work. Some people, some congregations, have developed this fatalistic assumption, built on a theology of low self-esteem, looking down on one's self, and thinking more poorly of one's self than one has a right to. Regrettably, people do this. Regrettably, congregations do this. They keep themselves in the tomb. They do not yet experience the grace of God, the Open Tomb, the Risen Lord, and New Life in Christ.

Something will work. We have confidence in the grace of God, the compassion of Christ, and the hope of the Holy Spirit.

You, the grassroots of your congregation, your key leaders, your pastor, and your staff can develop a helpful, excellent long-range plan. You can pool your deepest compassion, mutual wisdom, judgment, common sense, and prayer. You can focus on 20 percenters that deliver 80 percent of the results. You can give your most creative and constructive effort to developing a strong, healthy future. You do so out of the conviction that something will work.

Feel free to not expect everything to work. Frankly, not everything needs to work. A sufficient number of 20 percenter key objectives, working well, will grow forward the momentum and dynamic of your congregation. The art is to think through in a holistic, integrative, dynamic spirit your current strengths to expand and your new strengths to add. Expand and add these strengths in a way that creatively and constructively advances the whole. Do so, with the conviction that something will work.

I have served as consultant with congregations that, prior to my coming, had thirty-two losing years . . . . losing seasons. I have served as consultant with congregations that, in fact, border on the brink of the abyss, teetering on the edge, ready to fall into the chasm below. Many of these congregations have come to believe nothing will work.

I hold to the conviction that something will work because this conviction is important in the lives and destinies of people.

People lead in direct relation to the way they experience being led.

If you adopt the philosophy that nothing will work in your congregation, you have just taught every alcoholic in the congregation and in the community that nothing will work in his or her struggle with that human hurt and hope. If you adopt the attitude that nothing will work in your congregation, you have just taught every couple struggling with marriage problems in the congregation and the community that nothing will work.

If you adopt the perspective that nothing will work in your congregation, you have just taught every young person struggling with his or her own life's direction that nothing will work. Indeed, whenever the grassroots, key leaders, pastor, and staff of a congregation adopts the philosophy that nothing will work, it has just taught the people in that congregation and that community who are struggling with any specific hurt and hope that nothing will work in their lives as well.

If, after pooling all of the creative resources available to your local congregation, you still live the philosophy that nothing will work in this congregation, you have regrettably taught too many people that nothing will work in their own lives. If nothing will work in something as simple as growing forward a local congregation, then people regrettably conclude that nothing will work in something as complex as growing forward their lives and destinies.

It is far more decisive and helpful to share with people the spirit of the Gospel—something will work. The person struggling with alcoholism, the couple wrestling with their marriage, the young person thinking through the direction of his or her life's destiny, and all the people struggling with any specific hurt and hope benefit from the confidence that something will work in their own lives and destinies.

The reason something will work is not because of who we are and what we do, but because of whose we are and what God does. In Revelation 21:5 (RSV), we discover these words: *And God who sat upon the throne said, "Behold, I make all things new."*

The words do not say, "Behold, I make all things old." The words do not say, "Behold, I make all things the same." The words do not even say, "Behold, you/we make all things new." The words say, *"And God . . . said, 'Behold, I make all things new.' "*

Something will work. You can discern the ways God is inviting your congregation forward . . . . toward the future that God has both promised and is preparing for us. The reason something will work is because God takes a hand in the future and destiny of your congregation—and your life.

Something will work because God goes before the people as a cloud by day and as a fire by night, leading us through this present wilderness to the promised future. Something will work because we are the Easter People. We are the people of the Open Tomb, the Risen Lord, and New Life in Christ. With this conviction, we know that in our lives and in our congregation, something will work.

TEAM

The team includes you, the grassroots, the key leaders, the pastor, and the staff.

The "planning team" includes all of the people in the congregation. The whole congregation participates in creating the plan for your future. It is not as though a small committee, meeting almost privately, creates the plan for the future. Everyone who wants to is invited to help shape the plan.

Note that the title of this book is plural, not singular. It is the *Leaders' Guide,* not the *Leader's Guide.* It takes *a team* of people to develop a strong, healthy future for a congregation. The team includes you, the grassroots of your congregation, key leaders, your pastor, and staff. The team includes any resource leaders or consultants you invite to help your congregation.

The *Leaders' Guide* is written for you and the whole of your congregation. The principles and resources in it will help many people. Encourage a wide range of people—both grassroots and key leaders—to become familiar with this book as well as with *Twelve Keys to an Effective Church, Second Edition.*

When I wrote the original book, *Twelve Keys to an Effective Church*, I did not envision the extraordinary impact the book is having throughout the world. Moreover, I did not anticipate all the ways in which the principles in the original *Twelve Keys to an Effective Church* would contribute to many people in their work and business and in their everyday lives.

Again and again, as I have traveled throughout the planet, countless people have spoken to me of the insights the book has given them—in their congregation, in their work, and in their everyday life. Thus, as I have worked on this new *Twelve Keys Leaders' Guide,* I have kept these widespread applications fully in mind.

Invite a wide range of persons to study the new *Twelve Keys to an Effective Church.* Encourage many persons, both grassroots and key leaders, to study *The Twelve Keys Leaders' Guide.* Share together, across the whole congregation, in a prayerful study of *The Twelve Keys Bible Study.* Benefit from these three resources in whatever sequence is helpful to you and your congregation.

As you draw on these three resources, share with your congregation the three important ways the *Twelve Keys* books will help them.

1. The books help you to develop a strong, healthy future for your congregation.
2. The insights and principles help you with your work and business.
3. The possibilities and suggestions help in your everyday life—as you develop the sense of direction for your own life's pilgrimage.

The more people who are familiar with *The Twelve Keys* books, the stronger and healthier your future will be.

A CONGREGATIONAL SPIRIT

"We are family together." "We are in this together." "We have a congregational spirit." "We shape our future and live it out together."

All of the persons in the congregation as a whole, or as many who want to, are together the congregational planning team. We may have a planning steering team, consisting of five to eight persons. This steering team acts as a resource team and guides the congregation in the development of its effective long-range plan.

We share a congregational spirit as we share in:

Creative Study
Celebration Planning
Act Swiftly

Creative Study

With a congregational spirit, the more people who study the Twelve Keys books, the more helpful the plan. Involve as many grassroots persons and key leaders as possible. Invite members of the plan-ning team or a coaching consultant to guide the study. Do the study swiftly, over the shortest amount of time possible.

There is a tendency: the longer the study takes, the longer the planning takes. Invest a measured amount of time in the study. If you have to make a choice, invest more time in creative study and, then, the planning will move forward more swiftly. If you skip the study, or move too quickly through it, you will end up doing the study during the planning time. This will slow down the plan-ning and cause the action to be even slower.

Congregations do things at distinctive speeds. Match your study to the speed of your congregation.

There are congregations who do their creative study in board, session, or council meetings. They successfully study one or two of the **Twelve Keys** in their regular monthly meetings over a six- to twelve-month period. These congregations feel strongly that this plan of study is immensely helpful to them. This is so because these congregations tend to live life in this manner.

In our time, many congregations do their creative study in a more short-term, highly intensive manner. They may do their study in a congregation-wide Lenten study. They may do their study in a congregation-wide retreat or in small groupings across the con-gregation. They tend to live life in this manner. Think through the study plan that will work best for your congregation.

Celebration Planning

With a congregational spirit, the more we celebrate the strengths with which God is blessing us, the more likely we are to discover a strong, healthy future. The spirit with which we plan contributes to the future we achieve. In celebration planning, we begin with the gifts, strengths, and competencies with which God blesses us, however fragile we think they are.

Congregations who do "doom and gloom" planning deny the grace of God and the strengths with which God blesses them. Congregations who do "We are not certain this will work" planning create a timid, shy future. Congregations who do "harsh, demanding" planning create passive-aggressive behavior, low-grade hostility, subliminal resentment, and eruptive forms of anger.

Each person in the congregation celebrates the strengths God gives them, as persons. As a whole congregation, we celebrate the strengths with which God blesses us. We merge our individual strengths and our congregational strengths to shape our future.

Act Swiftly

With a congregational spirit, the more we act swiftly, the more we are likely to create a strong, healthy future.

We develop the motivational resources that help people move forward. We value the dynamics of memory, change, conflict, and hope that have major impact on any present moment and on any future moment in the life of the congregation. We build on the resources, possibilities, and participation principles that encourage congregations to act swiftly. We share the best practices that contribute to action, implementation, and momentum.

We study. We plan. We act swiftly. We share a congregational spirit.

11

CREATIVE STUDY

—

We develop a strong, healthy congregation with:

Creative Study
Celebration Planning
Act Swiftly

We look first at creative study.

WE LEARN IN MANY WAYS

We learn .... we have fun .... we act .... we live .... in a rich, full variety of ways. Study is *creative* when each of us draws on the distinctive ways with which each of us learns. Consider the ways you have fun, the ways you are creative, the ways you discover new possibilities. We learn in a vast variety of ways.

Some of us have a gift, a leaning, a propensity for learning in certain ways more than others. We can grow any of these ways of learning. For the moment, we have grown distinctive ways of learning. In the list below, look for the one or two ways of learning that match well with the ways in which you tend to learn.

Now, with this spirit of creative study, have fun with the new ***Twelve Keys to an Effective Church*** book.

Fun with athletic, physical ways. Many people learn in a physical, athletic way. Read the book as a playbook for a football, basketball, tennis, golf, or hockey team, or for whatever sport is fun for you. Look forward to developing a set of plays that will help your team share a winning season, and several winning seasons beyond.

Fun with intellectual, cognitive possibilities. Many people learn in a cognitive, intellectual way. Study this book as a text to map out a strategy plan for analyzing and developing a sequence of actions to advance the strengths and health for your congregation. Think of a chess match, a strategy game, a puzzle, or a mystery novel.

Fun with extracurricular, work projects. Many people learn in a work project manner. As they do a project, they learn. As you read *Twelve Keys,* look to create a blueprint of the project or projects you want to "construct" for your congregation. Organize the step-by-step "building plan" that completes the project. Think of a blueprint for shepherding or for mission, or for whichever strengths you want to advance.

Fun with social and relational ways. Many people learn in a person-centered, people-centered, relational, social manner. Enjoy *Twelve Keys* with a good-fun, good-times spirit. Think of a shower before a wedding. A great banquet. A good time. Create happy party discussions of the book. Have great fun in your planning retreat. Look forward to a wonderful wedding of grace and hope.

Fun with music and arts. Sing this book, looking for the melody, the tune, the rhythm of music that will help your congregation with its future way forward. Think of creating a picture or a painting, with shape and color values that match with the strengths of your congregation.

Enjoy *The Twelve Keys,* building on the specific ways of fun, learning, acting, and living that are helpful to you. Do your planning sessions with this same spirit. Live out your plan, act swiftly with this same spirit.

Listen for grace and goodwill. Listen for joy and good fun. Listen for your longings . . . . your yearnings . . . . your searchings . . . . your passion and compassion . . . . what you have fun doing.

WE STUDY WITH A HELPFUL SEQUENCE

Gather as many persons in the congregation as possible. Encourage your existing informal and formal groupings. Create several special study groupings. Invite as many persons as possible to study the new *Twelve Keys* book with good spirit and wisdom. Help them to know that the possibilities and principles they discover will help them in their business, their community, and their family life.

Share in a creative study of these *Twelve Keys* chapters:

Session 1: Grace, Strengths, Compassion
Session 2: Excellent Sprinters and Act Swiftly
Session 3: The keys that are strengths for your congregation
Session 4: The keys that are mid-range
Session 5: The keys that are likely weaknesses and the chapter
    on Mission, Sacrament, Grace

Some persons may want to study each of the *Twelve Keys* in its own study session. That is fine. Many congregations do their study over an extended period of time, giving thoughtful attention to each chapter in a specific study session. Solid marathon runners do this well.

Excellent sprinters tend to be more interested in *five sessions*. These five sessions may happen over a Friday evening and Saturday study retreat. They may happen with three sessions on one Saturday and two sessions on the next Saturday. They may take place once a week over five weeks.

We give each person their own book. They read the appropriate chapters before each study session. In each study session, we have excellent conversation and discussion. Beyond each session, persons frequently gather over coffee or tea for further conversation.

Study the new *Twelve Keys to an Effective Church* with this spirit and sequence.

1. We study the chapters on Grace, Strengths, and Compassion. We share in rich, full conversation about the wisdom and insights we discover in these chapters.

2. We read the Excellent Sprinters and Act Swiftly chapters. We discuss the possibilities for our congregation.

3. We study the chapters that discuss the keys that are likely our lead strengths. Look at the *Twelve Keys* chart. See the keys that "leap out" as strengths. Do not think about it too much. We are looking for our first impressions. It will come to us. "We do this one well." "We do this one well." Think of the keys we have fun doing. These are our lead strengths. As a congregation, we can come to a preliminary spirit as to our current strengths.

4. We read the chapters that discuss the keys that appear "mid-range" in terms of strength. We may do these keys *almost* well. They have some promise. On a scale of 1 to 10, they are a 5, 6, or 7.

5. We study the remaining chapters. These chapters discuss the keys that are a 1 to 4 on a scale of 1 to 10. These may be current weaknesses. We study the chapter on Mission, Sacrament, and Grace.

As we study *The Twelve Keys,* we may discover that what we thought was a weakness is, in fact, a mid-range, promising possibility. We may discover that what we thought was a current strength is, in fact, a mid-range or a weakness. We may discover that what we thought was a weakness is one of our strengths. We are open to new insights and new discoveries. We are looking for the strengths on which we can build our present and our future.

We are looking to:

Claim our strengths . . . .
Expand one or two current strengths . . . .
Add one or two new strengths . . . .
Sustain our current strengths . . . .
Act swiftly . . . .

We are open to the future to which God is inviting us.

The most helpful understanding of God in the Old Testament is of the God who goes before the people, as cloud by day and fire by night, leading them to the future which God is both promising and preparing for them.

The most helpful understanding of God in the New Testament is of the Open Tomb, the Risen Lord, and new life in the grace of God. The Risen Lord goes before us into Galilee . . . . into the mission. Have Fun . . . . Long for Grace . . . . Live in Grace . . . . Share Grace.

12

CELEBRATION PLANNING

We develop a strong, healthy congregation with:

Creative Study
Celebration Planning
Act Swiftly

We have looked at creative study. Now, let us look at celebration planning.

A SPIRIT OF CELEBRATION

We plan with a spirit of celebration. I call this celebration planning. We celebrate as we experience the grace God gives us and claim the strengths with which God blesses us. We claim our strengths. We rejoice. We discover one or two current strengths to expand. We give thanks. We discover one or two new strengths to add. We move forward.

We gather as many persons as we can. We share a spirit of anticipation. We look for excellent ideas and good suggestions. We want this to be a grassroots plan and a grassroots future. We want many persons to have ownership for the plan. The more people who participate in the planning, the more people who participate in the action.

The purpose of planning is action, not planning. We do just enough planning that we can move to the action . . . . swiftly . . . . with compassion and wisdom. We move forward in developing a strong, healthy congregation in the grace of God. We make course corrections as we move forward.

GRACE . . . . WITH THESE STEPS

We plan with grace. With the grace of God, we strengthen our congregation . . . . strengthen our lives. We stir our compassion. We draw close as community. We deepen our hope. We enjoy life. We discover our strengths. We live in the grace of God. We act swiftly. We advance our congregation with these steps:

> Claim your strengths.
> Expand one or two of your current strengths.
> Add one or two new strengths.
> Sustain your current strengths.
> Act swiftly on your present and future.

We sense the moving, stirring, encouraging grace of God in our lives and in our congregation. We benefit from the *Twelve Keys* chart. See Chapter Thirteen for this chart. We gather in a Twelve Keys Celebration Retreat. See the retreat schedule possibilities below. We discover our strengths. We expand and add our strengths. We act swiftly . . . . with the grace of God.

A TWELVE KEYS CELEBRATION RETREAT

We share in a *Twelve Keys Celebration Retreat*. We gather to shape our future. I have included two possible schedules. Feel free to benefit from either schedule or to develop one that matches with your congregation. The first schedule looks like this:

Our Twelve Keys Celebration Retreat

Our Congregational Gathering

We celebrate the grace with which God blesses us.
We look forward to sharing a good time together.
We have good fun as we pray and sing, plan and share.
We encourage everyone to come.

We plan for grace .... strengths .... compassion ....
mission ....
We share excellent ideas and good suggestions,
compassion and possibilities, wisdom and common sense.

We discover the strengths with which God blesses us.
We discover current strengths to expand.
We discover new strengths to add.
We sustain our current strengths.

We look for the strengths to expand and add to which God is
inviting us,
that we would have fun achieving, that are worthwhile,
and that stir our compassion, creativity, and hope.

We share a wonderful gathering, a family reunion.
We sing and pray.
We share simple, generous food.
We have a grand party, with joyful decorations.
We discover the future to which God is inviting us.
We enjoy good fun and fellowship.

8:00   Coffee, tea, water, juice, donuts, pastries, fruit

8:30   Welcoming, singing, praying

8:45   **Step 1: We claim our strengths.**
        Select your team partner. Decide your lead strengths
        among the **Twelve Keys.**

9:00   Find two other teams. Listen for their wisdom.
        Share your wisdom.
        As a small group, as best good friends can, decide
        which of the **Twelve Keys** are your current
        strengths.

9:30   We listen for the wisdom from the other small
        groups.
        As a small group, we share our wisdom with the
        whole gathering.

        As each group shares their wisdom, a leader, using
        "hash marks" on newsprint or an overhead, marks
        our current strengths.
        On our own **Twelve Keys** chart, we underline
        once the whole group's wisdom as to our current
        strengths.

        Singing, praying, thanksgiving for the strengths God
        gives our congregation.

10:00   Break – coffee, tea, water, juice, dessert, fruit

10:30   **Step 2: We expand one or two current strengths.**
        With your team partner, select one or two current
        strengths to expand that you know would be
        fun to achieve and would be a helpful gift to the
        community.

10:45   Find two other teams. Listen for their wisdom.
        Share your wisdom.
        As a small group, as best good friends can, decide
        which one or two of your current strengths would
        be fun to expand and would be helpful.

11:15   We listen for the wisdom from the other small groups.
         As a small group, we share our wisdom with the
         whole gathering.

> As each group shares their wisdom, a leader, using
> "hash marks" on newsprint or an overhead, marks
> our current strengths to expand.
> On our own *Twelve Keys* chart, we double
> underline the whole group's wisdom on the one
> or two current strengths to expand.

Singing, praying, thanksgiving for the strengths God
gives us to expand.

11:45   **Step 3: We add one or two new strengths.**
         With your team partner, select one or two new
         strengths to add.

12:00   Over lunch, find two other teams. Listen to their
         wisdom. Share your wisdom.
         As a small group, as best good friends can, decide
         which one or two new strengths we can add that
         we would have fun achieving and would help us to
         be a strong, healthy congregation.

1:15   We listen for the wisdom from the other small groups.
         As a small group, we share our wisdom with the
         whole gathering.

> As each group shares their wisdom, a leader, using
> "hash marks" on newsprint or an overhead, marks
> our new strengths to add.
> On our own *Twelve Keys* chart, we circle the
> whole group's wisdom on the one or two new
> strengths to add.

Singing, praying, thanksgiving for the strengths God
gives us to add.

1:45   Blessing

We have gathered and shared our compassion and wisdom . . . .
claimed the strengths God gives us . . . .
decided current strengths to expand . . . .
discovered new strengths to add . . . .
shared good fun and family together . . . .
sung and prayed,
asking God's blessing . . . .

We know where we are headed . . . . we give thanks to God.

The tradition we are beginning . . . .
is sharing gifts of grace each year
with our whole congregation.

A TWELVE KEYS CELEBRATION RETREAT—AN ALTERNATE SCHEDULE

An alternate schedule includes the encouraging statements in the opening and closing of the first schedule. It is built on a Friday night and Saturday time frame. This schedule has more extended times for conversation. It gives some "overnight thinking about it" time. Sometimes, this helps. Sometimes, it slows us down.

You will have the best wisdom as to what rhythm of schedule will be of help to you and your congregation. The second schedule looks like this.

Friday

6:00   Dinner . . . . We share a wonderful gathering, a
        family reunion.
        We begin with singing and praying. We share
        simple, generous food . . . .
        We have a grand party, with joyful decorations. We
        enjoy good fun and fellowship. With dessert,
        we share . . . .

7:00   **Step 1: We claim our strengths.**
        Select your team partner.
        Decide your lead strengths among the *Twelve Keys*.

7:30   Find two other teams. Listen for their wisdom.
        Share your wisdom.
        As best good friends can, as a small group, decide
        which of the *Twelve Keys* are your current
        strengths.

8:00   Break – coffee, tea, water, juice, dessert, fruit

8:30   We listen for the wisdom from the other small groups.
        As a small group, we share our wisdom with the
        whole gathering.

        As each group shares their wisdom, a leader, using
        "hash marks" on newsprint or an overhead, marks
        our current strengths.
        On our own *Twelve Keys* chart in our own book,
        we underline once the whole group's wisdom as
        to our current strengths.

8:50   Singing, praying, thanksgiving for the strengths God
        gives our congregation.

9:00   Blessing

Saturday

8:15   Coffee, tea, water, juice, donuts, pastries, fruit

8:30   Welcoming, singing, praying

8:45   **Step 2: We expand one or two current strengths.**
        With your team partner, select one or two current strengths to expand that you know would be fun to achieve and would be a helpful gift to the community.

9:15   Find two other teams. Listen for their wisdom. Share your wisdom.
        As a small group, decide which one or two current strengths to expand we would have fun achieving.

10:15   Break – coffee, tea, water, juice, donuts, fruit

10:45   We listen for the wisdom of the other small groups. As a small group, we share our wisdom with the whole gathering.

        As each group shares their wisdom, a leader, using "hash marks" on newsprint or an overhead, marks our current strengths to expand.
        On our own *Twelve Keys* chart in our own book, we double underline the whole group's wisdom on the one or two current strengths to expand.

11:15   **Step 3: We add one or two new strengths.**
        With your team partner, select one or two new strengths to add.

11:45   Find two other teams. Listen to their wisdom. Share your wisdom.
        As a small group, decide which one or two new strengths to add that we would have fun achieving.

12:15   Break

12:30   Over lunch, we listen for the wisdom of the other small groups.

We share our wisdom with the whole gathering.

> As each group shares their wisdom, a leader, using "hash marks" on newsprint or an overhead, marks our new strengths to add.
>
> On our own *Twelve Keys* chart in our own book, we circle the whole group's wisdom as to the new strengths to add.

1:15   Singing, praying, thanksgiving for the strengths God gives us to add.

1:30   Blessing

The first schedule gives fifteen minutes for team and small group conversations for claiming, expanding, and adding strengths. The alternate schedule gives thirty minutes for team and small group conversations. The first schedule concludes at 1:45 on Saturday. People make one trip for the planning retreat. The second schedule concludes at 1:30. People make two trips for the planning retreat.

In some congregations, the planning is done over several consecutive sessions during the regular Wednesday night congregational suppers. In some congregations, the planning is shared on Sunday mornings during church school. In others, the planning sessions are done on Sunday evenings as part of the special Sunday evening program.

Develop a planning schedule that works best for you and your congregation. Keep in mind that these planning steps—decisive in shaping the long-range future for your congregation—are best accomplished in concentrated planning sessions.

The spirit of the planning is more important than the schedule. The spirit is grace. The spirit is experiencing the grace of God . . . . celebrating the gifts and strengths with which God is blessing us. We rejoice. We give thanks. We are grateful. We look to the future which God is promising and preparing for us.

PERCEPTION

It is helpful for your congregation to develop a realistic and accurate perception of its strengths, gifts, and competencies. My formula is:

$$P > B > D.$$

Perception yields Behavior yields Destiny.

Fortunately, many congregations have a realistic perception of their strengths. Unfortunately, some congregations compare themselves with First Baptist or University Presbyterian and say, "We're not as big as they are." As a consequence, they tend to underestimate themselves.

Congregations grow forward or downward toward the strengths they claim, expand, add, and sustain. Inaccurate perception yields a frail, fragile future. This is one of the reasons we have weak and declining and dying congregations. Some congregations perceive themselves as weak and declining. They make "weak and declining" plans. Eventually, they grow themselves downward to weak and declining. Some congregations perceive themselves as dying congregations. They make "dying" plans. Their key objectives are in line with dying congregation standards. They create for themselves a dying future.

There is no merit in being bigger—to be bigger is to be bigger, not necessarily better. Some congregations romanticize bigness; and as a counter to that, other congregations romanticize smallness. "Thank God we are small and getting smaller." Some congregations say that because that confirms their own misperception of their future. There is no merit in being bigger or smaller.

The merit is to claim and celebrate the strengths with which God is blessing you. The merit is to expand a current strength and add a new strength. The merit is to act swiftly on your future. The reality is that God invites a congregation to share a mission commensurate with its present strengths.

13

ACT SWIFTLY

We develop a strong, healthy congregation with:

Creative Study
Celebration Planning
Act Swiftly

We have looked at creative study and celebration planning. Now, let us look at act swiftly.

EXCELLENT SPRINTERS

Excellent sprinters are drawn to groupings that act swiftly. The grassroots and the unchurched have a high density of excellent sprinters, including our own grandchildren. Increasingly, solid marathon runners are drawn to groupings that act swiftly. Many persons have learned both excellent sprinter and solid marathon runner patterns of behavior. People are no longer drawn to groupings that act slowly. We develop an action plan that moves swiftly.

Our *Twelve Keys* action plan may be a streamlined three pages long.

We claim our strengths. *page one*

On the *Twelve Keys* chart, we underline once our current strengths.

The chart is page one of our action plan.

We expand one of our current strengths.   *page two*

On page one, the **Twelve Keys** chart, we double underline the current strength we plan to expand.

On page two, we state the two to four specific key objectives that will expand this current strength. We may think of ten to fifteen possibilities. The art, what takes wisdom, is to select the two to four that are the 20 percenters. For each key objective, we state, as best we can, who will do what, by when, to achieve each objective.

We add one new strength.   *page three*

On page one, the **Twelve Keys** chart, we circle the new strength we plan to add.

On page three, we list the four to six key objectives that will add this new strength. We may think of ten, fifteen, or twenty possibilities. The art, the wisdom, is to select the four to six that will deliver this new strength. For each key objective, we state, as best we can, who will do what, by when, to achieve each objective.

Twelve Keys to an Effective Church
Strong, Healthy Congregations Living in the Grace of God

page one

Relational Characteristics

1. one mission outreach
by congregation in community
1　2　3　4　5　6　7　8　9　10

2. shepherding visitation
in congregation and community
1　2　3　4　5　6　7　8　9　10

3. stirring, helpful worship
grace centered, well done
1　2　3　4　5　6　7　8　9　10

4. significant relational groupings
home, roots, place, belonging
1　2　3　4　5　6　7　8　9　10

5. strong leadership team
leaders, pastor, staff
1　2　3　4　5　6　7　8　9　10

6. solid decision process
simple organization
1　2　3　4　5　6　7　8　9　10

Functional Characteristics

7. one major program
among best in community
1　2　3　4　5　6　7　8　9　10

8. open accessibility
in location and people
1　2　3　4　5　6　7　8　9　10

9. high visibility
in location and people
1　2　3　4　5　6　7　8　9　10

10. land, landscaping,
and parking
1　2　3　4　5　6　7　8　9　10

11. adequate space and facilities
spacious, well cared for
1　2　3　4　5　6　7　8　9　10

12. generous giving
solid financial resources
1　2　3　4　5　6　7　8　9　10

Claim your current strengths
Expand one current strength
Add one new strength
Act on your plan

underline strengths (8s, 9s, 10s)
underline a second time
circle a 1–7 to grow to an 8
decide your one-time actions

We expand one of our current strengths.   *page two*

We plan to expand this current strength _____

On the *Twelve Keys* chart, we double underline the current strength we plan to expand. On page two, we state the two to four specific key objectives that will expand this current strength.

Key Objective 1.

_____

_____

Key Objective 2.

_____

_____

Key Objective 3.

_____

_____

Key Objective 4.

_____

_____

We add one new strength. **page three**

We plan to add this new strength _____

On the *Twelve Keys* chart, we circle the new strength we plan to add. On page three, we list the four to six key objectives that will add this new strength.

Key Objective 1.

_____

_____

Key Objective 2.

_____

_____

Key Objective 3.

_____

_____

Key Objective 4.

_____

_____

Key Objective 5.

_____

_____

Key Objective 6.

_____

_____

Remember the Pareto principle: 20 percent of the things a group does delivers 80 percent of its results, accomplishments, and achievements. An objective that expands a current strength or adds a new strength is a key objective . . . . a 20 percenter.

DISCOVERING YOUR KEY OBJECTIVES

With your *Twelve Keys Celebration Retreat,* you now know the current strengths to expand and the new strengths to add. We act swiftly. We discover the key objectives with which to move forward our one expand and our one add. We gather a grouping of people for a one-time conversation.

The gathering has the spirit of an informal conversation with a team partner, a small grouping, and the larger gathering. The focus of the gathering is to discover the few key possibilities that will expand a current strength or add a new strength. We are looking for the possibilities to which God is inviting us.

Let us say we have decided to expand the key of stirring, helpful worship. We achieve two steps:

1. *We study the resources for stirring, helpful worship.*

You will find helpful, excellent ideas in **Dynamic Worship.** You will discover good suggestions in **Preaching for Grace, The Future That Has Come,** and **Twelve Keys for Living.** Encourage persons to select one or more of these resources to read and study before we gather for our conversation.

2. *We gather a grouping of people who are interested in expanding our current strength in worship.*

This is a one-time gathering. The gathering can include regular worshipers, occasional worshipers, Easter People, and community persons. It can include persons we hope would worship with us.

The gathering can include all the persons who have something to do with leading our service: parking greeters, ushers, music persons, worship leaders, and so on. Think of all the persons whose wisdom and experience would bring excellent ideas and good suggestions . . . . possibilities to expand our current strength in worship.

The schedule for our gathering might look like this:

8:00   Coffee, tea, water, juice, donuts, pastries, fruit

8:30   Welcoming, singing, praying . . . . with a joyful and grateful spirit

8:40   **Sharing our resources on stirring, helpful worship**

One or more resource persons lead a ten- to twelve-minute overview of each of the four major qualities of stirring, helpful worship:

> Our worship services are warm, winsome, and welcoming.
> Our music is inspiring and dynamic.
> The preaching is helpful and hopeful.
> Our service is stirring. It has balance, power, and movement.

The resource person may share his or her wisdom and invite persons in the gathering to share a discovery that has come to them in their study of these worship resources.

9:30   We discover our team partner. Our team partner is frequently the person sitting to our left or our right, whoever looks reasonably friendly, sort of half smiling, an intriguing, interesting person.

Together, the two of us come up with one excellent key possibility for worship that is creative and has value. We look at the four qualities of stirring, helpful worship:

> Our worship services are warm, winsome, and welcoming.
> Our music is inspiring and dynamic.
> The preaching is helpful and hopeful.
> Our service is stirring. It has balance, power, and movement.

We select one of these qualities. Then, together, we discover one key objective that will improve and advance this quality. We select one key objective that is most likely to expand our current worship strength, that we would have fun doing, and that would be helpful with people in their lives.

10:00   Break – coffee, tea, water, juice, desserts, fruit desserts, fruit

10:30   We find two other teams. We listen to each of their creative possibilities. We share ours. Together, as best good friends can, we decide the one key objective . . . . the one creative possibility we want to share with the whole group. Frequently, the one possibility from each team stirs yet a new, fourth possibility that has richer creativity and value.

11:00   We listen for the wisdom from the other small groupings.
As a small group, we share our wisdom with the whole gathering.
Someone lists, on newsprint or an overhead, each suggestion from each of the small groupings for the whole gathering to see.

> *Forty persons are twenty teams.*
> *Twenty teams are seven small groupings.*
> *We will have 7 excellent suggestions before us.*

11:20   Now, with your team partner, select the 4 out of the 7 we would have fun achieving in the near future.

> *"Yes" voting works this way.*
> *We take the total number of suggestions that have emerged.*
> *We find the halfway point and add one.*
> *For example, 7 suggestions emerge. 3 plus is the halfway point. Add 1. Each team selects the 4 of the 7 suggestions we would have fun achieving in the near future.*
> *If we had had a larger gathering and 10 suggestions had emerged, we would select 6 of the 10 suggestions.*

11:30   Find two other teams. Perhaps, the same two teams. Listen to each of their selections. Share yours. As a small group, as best good friends can, select the 4 of the 7 that will be most helpful and that we would have fun achieving.

11:45   The whole group listens to the 4 of 7 selections coming from each small grouping. Using hash marks, someone records the selections from the small groupings. We underline the major four.

         We do the 4 that have the deepest consensus.

         We save the other 3 for a later time.

         We act swiftly on the 4 now.

11:55   We give thanks to God. We give thanks for each person in this gathering.

         We sing. We share the blessing.

To expand a current strength, it takes two to four key objectives. We have discovered four. We do these four. We do, first, the two of the four that have the strongest interest with the whole gathering. Many of the persons who have participated in discovering the objectives will participate in achieving them.

We share in this same way to add a new strength. When we add a new strength, we look for four to six key objectives to grow forward.

For example, we might decide to add a new strength in shepherding visitation.

We would follow the same one-time gathering pattern discussed above.

1.   *We study the resources for shepherding visitation.*

    You will find helpful resources in ***A New Beginning for Pastors and Congregations, Visiting in an Age of Mission, The Future That Has Come,*** and ***Twelve Keys for Living.***

2. *We gather a grouping of people who are interested in adding a new strength in shepherding visitation.*

This is a one-time gathering. We would follow a schedule similar to the schedule above. We look at the four qualities of shepherding visitation:

> Our congregation shares immediate, generous shepherding visits with persons in hospitals, homebound, independent living, assisted living, and nursing homes.

> We share generous shepherding visits with our congregation: members, constituents, family and friends of our congregation.

> We share generous shepherding visits with our community: first-time worshipers, newcomers, friends in the community.

> Our shepherding visits have a sacramental quality benefiting and blessing people's lives.

We select one of these qualities. Then, we discover one key objective that will improve and advance the one quality we have selected. We select one key objective that would add this new strength in shepherding visitation, that we would have fun doing, and that would be helpful with people in their lives. We move forward with the steps outlined above.

In this process, our spirit is one of loving, listening, learning, and leading. We trust one another to be creative in ways that advance the whole. We value, look forward to, count on, and seek creative possibilities. We trust the creativity of the whole Body of Christ. We trust the creativity of God, moving, stirring, blessing us with grace and possibilities.

ACT SWIFTLY

We act swiftly. We move forward on our key objectives that are emerging, with this spirit:

1. This key objective is a creative, decisive action. It will make a substantial difference.

2. We will have fun achieving this objective. It stirs our wonder and joy, our love and compassion, our sense of new life and hope.
3. This objective builds on our strengths. It builds on what we do best.
4. This objective shows value and promise in serving and advancing God's mission.

We may be expanding a current strength in significant relational groupings. We might be adding a new strength in shepherding visitation. We could be expanding a current strength in open accessibility.

In each instance, we study the **Twelve Keys** resources that would help us. We look at the four qualities of each key. We gather a grouping to discover excellent ideas, good suggestions .... creative possibilities. We use the above *conversation process.* We act swiftly on our action objectives.

We share in a *Twelve Keys Celebration Retreat.* We discover our strengths, one to expand, and one to add. We share in a *gathering conversation* for the one we will expand and for the one we will add. We encourage many persons to participate in the celebration retreat and in the conversations. We do just enough planning that we can head to the action.

We study. We celebrate. We discover possibilities. We act swiftly. We develop a strong, healthy congregation.

MATCHES, TIMELINES, FOCUS

MATCHES

We are looking for strengths that are matches with one another. We want a match among the current strength(s) we are expanding and the new strength(s) we are adding. When we select a current strength to expand, we choose one of our strongest strengths. When we select a new strength to add, we pick a key among the twelve that is "mid-range." It is a 5, 6, or 7 on a scale of 1 to 10.

We do not select our weakest weakness, something that is a −49 on a scale of 1 to 10. We look for a possibility, among the twelve, that has some good-fun, helpful promise of becoming a new strength.

We might decide to expand a second current strength that matches with and helps both "expands" to grow forward together. Expanding a current strength in worship and a current strength in parking is a helpful match. Expanding a current strength in shepherding and a current strength in generous giving is a helpful match. The art is to expand two strengths that reinforce and help one another.

We might decide to add a second new strength. We would add a second new strength that matches with and helps the one or two we are expanding and the one new strength we are adding. We might decide to:

expand one current strength   add one new strength

or

expand a current strength   add a new strength
expand a second current strength

or

expand a current strength   add a new strength
expand a second current strength   add a second new strength

Or, we may discover some other combination to which we sense God is inviting us.

Likewise, we are looking for key objectives that are matches with one another. We want key objectives that help us to head in the same direction. We want key objectives that:

1. Stir our compassion
2. Stretch our strengths
3. Encourage our creativity
4. Are realistic and achievable
5. Have solid time horizons
6. Are led by a competent team
7. State who will do what, by when
8. Match with one another

All of these are central to having solid key objectives. Many congregations include all eight of these qualities in developing their key objectives.

Some congregations have difficulty with the eighth one above: key objectives that match with one another. Some congregations are prone to head in several directions with their key objectives. They have a tendency to "scatter" in multiple directions. Sometimes, this "scattering" is caused by a dubious desire to please everyone. Sometimes, it is the result of a "department" or "silo" mentality. Sometimes, it is simply a lack of practice in the art of focusing on a few, matching key objectives.

Your congregation has a better opportunity to be strong and healthy as you focus on strengths and key objectives that are matches with one another.

TIMELINES

We look three years ahead. We do so in a swift, dynamic, developmental spirit, not in a slow, rigid, block manner. We discussed this approach in Chapter Nine. Life moves too swiftly in our time to do that slow, rigid, block approach.

On some matters, we may look thirty to forty years ahead. We do so when we consider location, land, and facilities. We do so when we consider our long-range mission, shepherding, worship, and groupings future. Sometimes, we look three weeks and three months ahead. See my book *A New Beginning for Pastors and Congregations,* which focuses on a three-month new beginning. Mostly, we look three years ahead in strength-building, strategic, operational ways.

As you develop timelines, keep these principles in mind:

1. Timelines develop confidence and competence. Focus on those key objectives that encourage the confidence and competence of the congregation. It is easier to expand a current strength than it is to add a new strength. The congregation is more likely to tackle tough, hard problems when its confidence and competence have been developed.

The congregation is more likely to become tense and tight and to resist tackling tough problems when persons feel they have been set up to fail. The art is to grow forward the confidence and competence of the congregation.

Many congregations make the mistake of loading the first year of their plan with more than they can accomplish in that year.

Then, they tend to be vague about the middle year of their plan and "hope to have everything accomplished by the last year."

It is most important that there be a workable set of timelines demonstrating a reasonable pace and work flow that the leaders and grassroots of the congregation can substantially achieve and accomplish.

2. Expand first those strengths that are easiest to expand. When you develop the first year of your plan, if you have a choice between expanding a current strength and adding a new one, the better choice is to expand a current strength.

In the first year, you set up your congregation to succeed, not fail. Remember this principle: build on your strengths— do better what you do best. Successfully expanding a current strength puts you in a stronger position to add a new strength in the future.

3. Develop a natural rhythm. Select the combination of expands and adds and related key objectives that will develop a natural rhythm of momentum and a natural dynamic of swift action for your congregation. The sequential character of specific key objectives is unique for each congregation.

4. Develop complementary priorities. Develop timelines that coordinate complementary priorities in the same years. They mutually reinforce one another.

One congregation announced it had two key objectives for the coming year: (1) to reach twenty new unchurched young couples with small children, and (2) to build the choir's community-wide reputation for excellence by singing only classical music during the service of worship. These were two excellent objectives. But they were not complementary priorities for that same year.

Radio marketing surveys in the community indicated that young couples listened to two kinds of music: soft rock FM and country-western. To help these objectives to more fully complement one another, the music leaders increased the choir's reputation by preparing well and singing two special community concerts of classical music each year, and they kept to middle-of-the-road anthems during the Sunday services. They initiated child care during choir rehearsals. They attracted some of the new young couples to the choir.

Think through your timelines so that complementary priorities mutually reinforce one another during each year of your plan.

FOCUS ON STRENGTHS

The art is to focus. We focus on the strengths we plan to expand, add, and sustain. Some congregations create a simple mission statement that gathers the focus of where the congregation is heading and what it hopes to achieve.

First, we discover the strengths we plan to expand, add, and sustain. Then, we summarize our sense of direction in a helpful, encouraging mission statement. It is not that we create a mission statement, then decide which keys to expand and add. We grow our mission statement up from the grassroots, not the top down.

The *Twelve Keys* planning steps are built on grassroots participation, with team partners, small groupings, the whole congregation, and the spirit of "Yes" voting.

We gather in grace and hope. We share our compassion, our sense of family and community, and our wisdom and understanding. We have a deep sense of our possibilities. We are earnest, thoughtful, and forward thinking. We see, more fully, the persons we are serving. We feel, more deeply, the future to which God is inviting us.

We sense the grace with which God blesses us. We share fellowship, fun, and family together. We sing and pray. We ask God's blessing. We give thanks to God for the grace with which God blesses us. We are grateful for the compassion with which God surrounds us. We give thanks for the hope with which God leads us. We look forward to where we are headed. We live in grace and hope.

We share and plan, celebrate and pray . . . . with a good-fun, good-time spirit, thoughtfully, deliberately, with a mixture of singing and laughing, worshiping and praying. We discover excellent ideas and good suggestions. We involve the whole congregation.

There is conversation . . . . creativity . . . . discovery. We discover possibilities that advance our whole congregation and are well matched with the mission field God gives us. We claim the strengths God gives us. We discover the current strengths we plan to expand and the new strengths we plan to add.

CONCLUSION: GRACE

Congregations are people. One cannot have a congregation without people. People create congregations. Congregations are a rich mix of people with a diversity of strengths, interests, longings, and hopes. When people come to a congregation, they bring with them all of who they are.

Strong, healthy congregations are created by:

Grassroots persons, key leaders, and pastors
Momentum, resources, and strengths
The world
The grace of God

Wherever we discover a congregation that is strong and healthy, effective and successful, we will find these four gifts in place.

GRASSROOTS, KEY LEADERS, AND PASTORS

God blesses congregations with the whole family of God. Grassroots persons, key leaders, and pastors create strong, healthy congregations. *There was an early myth that a pastor could create a strong congregation.* This myth led to the notion of the "celebrity" pastor, the dynamic, charismatic leader who would draw many followers. It was an interesting notion.

One difficulty is that most pastors are not "celebrity leaders." When they try to be one, it gets them "off of their game." They try to be someone they are not. They lose who they really are. The charade comes across as artificial and awkward. They feel tense and tight, nervous and anxious. They do not feel like natural, warm, open, and inviting persons. They feel stilted and busy.

The further difficulty is that most effective CEOs are not "celebrity leaders." If pastors could bring off being "celebrity pastors," the irony is that it still would not work. Jim Collins, in his research for his book *Good to Great,* discovered that effective, successful CEOs have three qualities in common: a deep humility, a passion for the mission, and a capacity to work with a team.

We do not hear about them because of their deep humility. We do not hear about countless compassionate, competent pastors because of their deep humility. They quietly go about the work of being:

a good shepherd
a helpful preacher
a wise, caring leader
a community pastor

They were drawn to the ministry because of their desire to help and serve, not so they could be noticed and notarized. They were drawn to helping people.

Somewhere along the way, the myth emerged that it takes a pastor and key leaders to create a strong, healthy congregation. Many workshops were held. Many pamphlets were written. Many resources were distributed. The message was, "When the pastor and the key leaders work together, they will create a successful church." It did not happen. It does not happen.

Oh, for a spurt of time, the pastor and the key leaders can move some things forward. Over the long haul, it does not last. A general and some officers do not make an army. An admiral and some bridge officers do not make a navy. A coach and an offensive captain and a defensive captain do not make team.

A quilting expert and a quilting council do not make a quilting group. A concert master and a pianist do not make an orchestra. You will think of many comparable examples.

In some denominations, the gap between the denominational leaders and the pastors is one hundred yards. The gap between the pastors and the key leaders is three hundred yards. Much to-do is made of these two gaps. Many efforts are tried, with sincerity and diligence, to close these two "horrendous" gaps. There is much embarrassment over these two gaps. "Our problems will be over when we close these two gaps."

The reason there is such an emphasis on these two gaps is because the only people in the room, in many settings, are the denominational leaders and the pastors. In many other settings, the only people in the room are the pastors and the key leaders.

The people who are not in the room are the grassroots.

The grassroots are all of the members, constituents, persons served in mission, community persons, and family and friends of your congregation. They are not the key leaders. They are not the chairs of committees. They are not the council or the session. Most of them participate in some informal shepherding grouping. Most of them come to worship, some regularly, some frequently, some on Christmas Eve and Easter.

If the gap between the denominational leaders and the pastors is one hundred yards, and the gap between the pastors and the key leaders is three hundred yards, *the gap between the key leaders and the grassroots is one thousand yards.* The first gap is one football field long. The second gap is three football fields long. The third gap is ten football fields long. Many suggest it is farther than that.

God gives your congregation a whole family of God. God gives you three gifts: grassroots persons, key leaders, and a pastor and staff. The reality is that it takes a combination, a team, of grassroots persons, key leaders, and a pastor to create a strong, healthy congregation. Any two of the three have difficulty.

God gives you a fourth gift . . . . all of the persons in the community God is inviting you to serve in mission. Finally, all four gifts create a strong and healthy, effective and successful congregation. Without this fourth gift, we do not have the possibility of being a congregation in service and mission.

Some pastors and key leaders ask this question, "Why us?" The inference in the question is,

> We are almost able to get along as pastor and key leaders. You want us to *fool with* the grassroots. You want us to *fool with* serving persons in the community?
> We can almost agree with one another. You want us to listen and learn from the grassroots and the community?

I gently answer, "Yes, you have it. We love, listen, learn, and lead together as a team, as the whole Body of Christ. We are in this together."

Every movement is grown from the grassroots up, not the top down. Every healthy congregation is grown from the grassroots up, not the top down. One good friend and I were having lunch. He had been elected a bishop some several months before. He said to me, "Ken, I am having a tough time. Turning this denomination around is like turning a Queen Elizabeth ocean liner. You turn it slowly."

I said,

> My good friend, a denomination is not a Queen
> Elizabeth ocean liner. A denomination is a flotilla, a fleet,
> a convoy of many ships of different shapes and sizes. The
> art is to help this ship, then this ship, then this ship to see
> the new course. The rest of the fleet begins to see the
> new way. You turn any movement from the grassroots.

> The same is true in a congregation. A congregation is
> a collection, a grouping, a gathering of many people of
> distinctive strengths and longings. The art is to help this
> person, this grouping, this gathering to discover the new
> way forward. It takes grassroots persons, key leaders, and a
> pastor to grow forward a strong, healthy congregation.

This note is helpful for pastors. Some congregations have an informal pastor who is a good shepherd; a helpful preacher; a wise, caring leader; and a community pastor. This informal pastor has an informal degree from the seminary of life. She or he may not have a Master of Divinity degree from a formal seminary. This person does deliver the primary gifts and competencies of a pastor.

I have earned four degrees. I have had the privilege of teaching on the faculty of one of the most extraordinary seminaries on the planet. I value education and competencies, standards and requirements. My standards are considerably higher than most. And, on occasion, I have been known to say, "If someone has a Master of Divinity degree, I do not hold that against them. But what are in their favor are their competencies, not their credentials."

There are countless congregations across the planet with an informal pastor, who has never been to a formal seminary. These congregations flourish and do good work. They deliver three of the five basic qualities of a strong, healthy congregation. They prosper. They serve in mission. They deliver nine of the twelve keys of effective, successful congregations. They help people with their lives and destinies. They live in the grace of God.

This note is helpful for persons with the gifts of being an administrator. I have deep admiration and appreciation for persons who have the competencies of an administrator. It works very well for a minister to have the gifts of being primarily an administrator when one of two things is true:

1. It is a church culture, where congregations have many busy programs and activities that invite the need for a gifted, competent administrator.
2. Other persons in the congregation or on the staff deliver the gifts and competencies of being a good shepherd; a helpful preacher; a wise, caring leader; or a community pastor; or, at least, three of these four competencies.

Many healthy congregations have informal key leaders who glue the venture together and help the congregation move forward. The formal key leaders of the committees and task forces may deliver mediocre to mid-range solid work. When we look closely, it is the excellent work of the informal shepherding key leaders who deliver the momentum. They are the informal key leaders of the informal shepherding groupings of the congregation. With their informal leadership, the congregation is strong and healthy.

Likewise, it is the strengths, gifts, and competencies of grassroots persons who contribute to a congregation being strong and healthy. With the grassroots, congregations serve persons well. Lives and destinies are deepened and advanced. The mission moves forward.

MOMENTUM, RESOURCES, AND STRENGTHS

God blesses congregations with momentum, resources, and strengths. Momentum, resources, and strengths create strong, healthy congregations. Demotivation, complaining, and weaknesses create weak, declining, and dying congregations. We have invested much of this book on moving forward with your momentum, building on your resources, and developing your strengths. These three create strong, healthy congregations.

Preoccupations

Three preoccupations distract a congregation from its momentum, resources, and strengths. A preoccupation with *demotivation* does not draw people to a congregation. People receive enough demotivation in day-to-day living. They are not interested in becoming part of a congregation that is filled with demotivation. People look for, long for groupings that will encourage them with the motivations of compassion, community, hope, challenge, reasonability, and commitment.

They are not interested in the demotivations of anxiety, fear, anger, and rage. They do not long for passive-aggressive behavior, low-grade hostility, subliminal resentment, and eruptive forms of anger. They do not yearn for resentment, bitterness, grudges, and guilt.

They are not interested in quiet, well-mannered, speaking softly persons who tell them they can "do better." They long for someone who will bless them . . . . who will stir their compassion, community, and hope.

Similarly, a preoccupation with *complaining* does not draw people to a congregation. In day-to-day life, some persons develop their gifts for complaining, bemoaning, lamenting, grumbling, whining, and whinging. These are their good friends. They go everywhere with the person.

One can almost see these good friends prancing and dancing alongside the person, holding hands, gleefully and cheerfully. The person transports them everywhere. They can only get somewhere if the person takes them. And, the person has come to "enjoy" their company. They are happy to share their complaining spirit wherever the person takes them. When the person comes to church, the person brings all of these good friends with them.

It is not that they live life with a grace-filled and joyful spirit, and, then, have a complaining spirit only in their church. They share their gift for complaining wherever they are . . . . family, work, common interests, community, and church. They are not selective. They are simply this way everywhere, with everyone. And, people are not drawn to congregations that have a complaining spirit. They are drawn to congregations that are building on the resources with which God is blessing them.

Likewise, a preoccupation with *weaknesses* does not encourage a congregation . . . . or a person. People are not drawn to congregations preoccupied with weaknesses. People have enough difficulty claiming their strengths and building on them. They do not want the "distraction" of a preoccupied perfectionism that leads them away from their strengths.

People, intuitively and instinctively, sense that one builds a healthy life on the strengths with which God blesses them. They sense that congregations do the same. They do not shy away from their weaknesses. They began with their strengths. They build on what they do best.

God blesses congregations who focus on their momentum, resources, and strengths.

Coaching

Frequently, a congregation benefits from coaching. The many books in the *Twelve Keys Library of Resources* provides a wealth of possibilities. Many congregations move forward with the benefits of this library. The new *Twelve Keys* book, the new *Leaders' Guide,* and the new *Bible Study* encourage congregations to grow forward with their own initiative, creativity, leadership, and planning. They develop a strong, healthy future.

Many congregations value the resources of a coaching person or team. This is especially true with congregations that are doing well and want to advance their strengths and mission. Your congregation may well benefit from this coaching.

Coaching is coaching, not correcting. Coaching is encouraging, not discouraging. Coaching helps a congregation to deepen its momentum, build on its resources, and develop its strengths. Coaching helps in several ways. A coaching person:

> leads the congregation in a study of *Twelve Keys to an Effective Church, Second Edition*
>
> leads the congregation in its **Twelve Keys Celebration Planning Retreat**
>
> leads the congregation in using *The Twelve Keys Bible Study*
>
> works alongside the congregation in the early stages as it acts swiftly on its new long-range plan

There are numerous persons who have developed their coaching competencies in one or more of these areas. These coaching persons are very familiar with the **Twelve Keys** resources. They bring in-depth experience and expertise in the **Twelve Keys** principles. They lead congregations in one or all four of these coaching areas. They help a congregation to include the whole congregation—grassroots persons, key leaders, pastor, and staff—in developing a strong, healthy future.

In addition, a coaching consultant coaches grassroots persons, key leaders, pastors, and staff to become deeply familiar with the **Twelve Keys** materials and principles. They emerge as resident resource persons with their own congregation and with other congregations in their area. The coaching consultant grows new coaches. The coaching consultant helps a congregation to develop its creativity and motivation, self-sufficiency and self-reliance, self-direction and leadership to achieve objectives for which it has strong ownership.

A coaching consultant shares his or her best compassion and wisdom, experience and judgment, common sense and prayer. He or she shares possibilities that help. The coach helps the congregation to discover excellent ideas and good suggestions that are present within the congregation. The coaching consultant encourages a mutual sharing of wisdom and hope.

The consultant shares his or her best mutual wisdom and judgment, vision and common sense, and does so in a prayerful, compassionate, coaching way.

We deepen our momentum. We build on our resources. We grow forward our strengths. We avoid preoccupations. We benefit from a coach. We grow forward a strong, healthy congregation.

THE WORLD

God blesses congregations with the world. The world creates strong, healthy congregations.

The center of grace is the world, not the church. Jesus is born in a world of mission. Grace is grassroots. Jesus is born in a manger, not a mansion. Jesus is born in a stable, not a castle.

Jesus is born in cattle stall, not a cathedral. Shepherds and wise men gather, not princes and kings. Grace is for everyday, ordinary people who are born, live, and serve in the world, blessed by the grace of God.

The church was born in a world of mission . . . . in one of the richest ages of mission the world has ever seen. Welcome to the first century. Welcome to the twenty-first century. Welcome to the Mission Growth Movement. Welcome to the Twelve Keys Movement. Welcome to one of the greatest ages of mission the world has ever seen.

God gives us this new world of mission we now have so we can remember where we were born. We were not born in sacred halls or lofty churches. We were not born in committee meetings and organizational structures. We were not born among tricks and trivialities. God gives us this new world of mission so we can grow forward our best, true selves, our deepest momentum, our stirring compassion and passion, our thoughtful wisdom, and our helpful strengths . . . . to serve in the world.

Grace is in the world. Whenever the church is in the world, grace is in the church. Whenever the church is not in the world, grace is in the world. The text is not, "For God so loved the church . . ." The text is, "For God so loved the world . . ." (John 3:16, RSV). God does not forsake the world to save the church. God invites the church to be *in* the center of people's lives, not to be the center of their lives.

The church is not the center of grace. The world is the center of grace. In that long lost church culture, we lived as though the church was the center of grace. The church is never at its best in a church culture. In a church culture, the church becomes bloated and bureaucratic, lazy and indifferent. The church waits on the culture to deliver people to it. It assumes that because it is "the thing to do to go to church," people will find the church of their own initiative and volition.

God gives us this wondrous new world of mission to teach us that the world is the center of grace. For a long, long time, almost from the beginning of time, people believed the earth was the center of the universe. As humankind looked out to the stars, one could simply see that the earth is the center.

Nicolaus Copernicus was born February 19, 1473. He passed away on May 24, 1543, at seventy years of age. His major work, *De revolutionibus orbium coelestium* (*On the Revolutions of the Celestial Spheres*) was published in 1543 just before he died. You will want to note that Nicolaus was forty-four years old when Luther published his ninety-five theses in 1517 that launched the Protestant Reformation.

Copernicus had two insights: one, the earth is in daily motion on its axis; and two, the earth is in yearly motion around a stationary sun. His heliocentric understanding has the sun at the center. The earth is no longer the center of the universe.

There were ancient murmurings to the contrary, but the prevailing view in Copernicus's time, held for centuries upon centuries, was that the earth was the center of the universe. This earth-centric view of the universe pervaded all of life. Earth is the center of the universe. Humankind is the center of the universe. The structures of humankind are the center of the universe. The Church is the center of the universe. This had been the view.

Added to this, with the fall of Rome in 410 A.D., there was an emerging sense, at least in the West, that the Church was the center of humankind, and, therefore, the center of the universe. It was the case that the Church increasingly had to take upon itself much of the ordering and structuring of life. For centuries, merchants had sailed and armies had marched to the banner, "Rome Is Eternal." With the fall of Rome, Augustine, Bishop of Hippo, developed his theology around the banner, "The City of God Is Eternal."

With Copernicus, 1,133 years later, the insight emerges that the earth is not the center of the universe. The implication is that humankind is not the center of the universe. The implication is the church is not the center of the universe. The implication is the church is not the center of humankind.

This discovery encourages us to be *in* the center of people's lives, not the center of their lives. The earth is not the center.

The church is not the center. The grace of God is the center. Our banner is, "The Grace of God Is Eternal."

God invites the church to be in the center of people's lives. God encourages us to live as mission congregations. God richly blesses us. We live on one of the richest mission fields on the planet. God invites us to this new day. We no longer live in the church culture of the 1950s. The day of the busy, bustling post–World War II suburban church as the center of people's lives is over. The day of the mission congregation has come.

The world is the center of the mission. A few pastors and key leaders still behave as though Copernicus had never lived. Copernicus helped us to see that the earth is not the center of the universe. Likewise, the church building is not the center of life. Just because a few people and a few pastors decided to make the church building the center of their lives does not mean that everyone should.

In some ways, the notion that the church should be the center of life is an archeological relic left over from that ancient time when the earth was thought to be the center of the universe and the church, therefore, thought it should be the center of life. In this new day, some pastors and key leaders will want to rethink God's calling for them—was it to a church building or to a mission? A few pastors think their place of work is in their office. Not so. Their place of work is in the world.

A pastor, recently graduated from seminary, took up his post at his first congregation. Upon his arrival, his first two questions were, "Where is my office?" and "When is my first meeting?" These two questions are archeological relics left over from the church culture of the 1950s. In this new day, the best first two questions are, "Who is our mission?" and "Who are our people?"

It is understandable that a few pastors and key leaders want the church to be the center of every person's life. These people have decided to make the church the center of their lives. Therefore, it is natural they would want others to share the same commitment. But the premise is the problem. Pastors are not called to make the church the center of their lives. Pastors are called to make God's mission the center of their lives.

Fortunately, we have come to a time when many pastors know they have been called to serve a mission field—a whole community—not solely a church building or members only. We have come to a time when many congregations know their focus is to serve persons in the community, not to get people in the community to serve that church.

The focus of the congregation is not the church building. The focus of the church is the world. God is in the world. Whenever the church is *in* the world, God is in the church. Whenever the church is not in the world, God is not in the church. God has planted us on one of the richest mission fields on the planet. Just when some of us had begun to think life was almost half over and all we had to do was to stay out of major trouble until the end, God has given us a new day. God invites us to share the grace of God in the world.

In this new day, long-range plans do not look like those we used to develop in that long-ago, almost fully extinct church culture. Now, they look like the plans of a people on a mission field. In this new day, we focus more on mission and compassion than on membership and maintenance. We do not press people to spend more time at church. We help people invest their time in the world, sharing the compassion and competencies with which God blesses them.

Our "statistical goals," the columns in our annual reports, include, focus on, and look like:

The number of persons we have served in
mission this past year   _____

The number of persons we look forward to
serving in mission this coming year   _____

The focus is on mission, not membership.

A few congregations continue to behave as though this were still the church culture of the 1950s. They do one thing very well. They successfully become weak and declining or dying congregations. A pastor or key leader who still behaves as though it were the post–World War II church culture of the 1950s can be compared to the captain on the bridge of a disabled ship. He or she presides, with honor and dignity, as the ship slowly founders and sinks into the depths of the sea beneath. Or, such a key leader or pastor can be compared to a noble undertaker who, with decorum, dignity, and thoughtfulness, presides over a quiet funeral.

When the church seeks to be the center of people's lives, it is no different from the other entities of our culture that clamor to gain central place in people's lives. When the church decides to be in the center of people's lives, the church transcends the entities of the culture. It gives up its own self-seeking, survival-oriented tendencies. It becomes an entity focused on compassion and serving, sharing, and caring. Whenever the church does this, the church is truly the church.

In an earlier time, it may have been possible to get away with developing long-range plans that focused on membership and maintenance. No more. The day of membership and maintenance is over. The day of mission and compassion has come.

Whether a given local congregation survives or not is in God's hands. Some of our churches will one day be footnotes in the dusty books of church history. Be at peace. We are called to serve, not to endure. God encourages us to focus on service, not survival. God invites us to be in the center of people's lives, serving human hurts and hopes. God encourages us to a mission of reconciliation, wholeness, caring, and justice. God calls us not to seek survival but to share service.

One can read a church bulletin or a church newsletter and sense whether the congregation is sharing service, or is preoccupied with survival. One can listen to a sermon and sense where the pastor's concern is. One can sit in a meeting and sense the preoccupation of that congregation. In some meetings, it is a regular practice to share information on who has moved and who has died this past month. Hardly ever is it a regular practice to share information on who has been helped in mission this past month or who has discovered the grace of God this past month.

If you want to worry, worry about something that counts. To worry about whether your local congregation will survive is to worry about a lesser thing. To worry for the human hurts and hopes of the many people who have yet to discover the grace of God—now this is a worry worth worrying about. This is a worry that counts!

We spend too much time trying to get people to come to the church building. We can invest more time being the church with the people in the world. It used to be said many times (and with considerable pride), "We were there every time the doors of the church were open." In our time, it is said of mission congregations, "We were there to help when a person experienced hurt and hope." The locus of the congregation in a church culture is the church building. The focus of the congregation on a mission field is at the front lines of human hurts and hopes, where people are born, live, and die . . . . where people long for grace.

We have lived though extraordinary times. We have gone from one age to the next. We have seen, now one banner and, then, the next banner prevail:

Rome Is Eternal
The City of God Is Eternal
The Grace of God Is Eternal
The Mission of God Is Eternal

The banners of grace and mission now fly. The world God now gives us invites the banners of grace and mission. Thanks be to God.

There is an ancient document, now and then found at hotels and motels. On rare occasions, someone opens the long lost manuscript and discovers these quietly powerful words:

If any person would come after me,
let that person deny himself
and take up his cross and follow me.
For whoever would save his life will lose it,
and whoever loses his life for my sake will find it.

Matthew 16:25 (RSV)

This text applies to congregations as well as to individuals. Live this passage in your own life. Encourage your congregation to live this passage in its life.

If any congregation would come after me,
let that congregation deny itself
and take up its cross and follow me.
For whatever congregation would save its life will lose it,
and whatever congregation loses its life for my sake will find it.

Matthew 16:25 (RSV, paraphrased)

Mission congregations are congregations of service.

Your congregation is a sacred trust given to you by God. Your congregation is a sacrament . . . . a living, breathing, moving, sharing, serving sacramental grouping of grace, compassion, community, and hope. Your congregation is sacrament of mission and grace.

THE GRACE OF GOD

God blesses congregations with grace. The grace of God creates strong, healthy congregations.

We live with deep humility in the presence of the grace of God. We are amazed at the generous grace of God. We do not boast. We do not brag. We do not call attention to ourselves. We are humble. We share wonder and joy that we live in the grace of God.

We give thanks. We are humbly grateful. We live with humility.

We live in grace. The grace of God blesses us with momentum. The grace of God blesses us with resources for strengthening our congregation. The grace of God helps us in developing the strengths of our congregation.

"The grace of God be with you." This blessing confirms God's grace surrounds you and sustains you. God gives you the gift of life. God blesses you with gifts, strengths, and competencies. God blesses you with compassion, community, and hope. God invites you to the future God has promised and is preparing for you.

"The Force be with you." This recent, interesting saying has in mind some unknown force, somewhat strange and alien, inscrutable and immutable, hard to discern, hard to find. The notion is that this force pervades and dominates the universe. When you align with the Force, you will have power. You will have strength. You will prevail.

In Athens, Paul shares with the people of his time that the Unknown God they have been worshiping is, in fact, the God of grace revealed in Jesus Christ. If you have had any tendency or, indeed, temptation to think of the universe as being pervaded by an "unknown force," feel free to know that the universe is pervaded by the grace of God. We are not moved and shaped by some unknown force. That notion is an ancient notion. We are blessed and encouraged with the grace of God.

We are who we are with the grace of God. We are who we can be with the grace of God. Wherever the grace of God is, there is compassion, community, and hope.

The stars are the sacramental sign of the immensity of God's grace. God creates the universe as immense as it is so we know how immense God's grace is for us. The manger is the sacramental sign of the immediacy of God's grace. God wants us to know how near, how immediate God's grace is for us.

As you decide your future plan, you are deciding how your life will count. Most persons want their lives to count. Your life will count more as you invest it in mission and compassion.

On a mission field, many persons invest their lives in the world more than in the church. Some may protest tentatively that this is too idealistic. Not so. Whoever would suggest that is the idealist, is still living in the church culture of the 1950s. I am being the realist, not the idealist. We live on a mission field. Our effective long-range plan takes this fact realistically and seriously.

Discover, develop, and decide the long-range plan that matches best with your current strengths and the community—the mission field—your congregation seeks to serve. Live out your plan with action, implementation, and momentum.

My hope is that your plan will not generate more programs and activities, more meetings and maintenance, more committees and agencies. Rather, my hope is that your plan will generate:

Mission teams, the likes of which your community and the world have not yet seen

Shepherding visitation teams that deliver sharing and caring with persons served in mission, constituents, and members

Worship and prayer teams that give the world, your community, and your congregation a new spirit of compassion and hope

Groupings in which persons discover roots, place, belonging, family, and home

Leaders who lead with compassion and wisdom, who plan well, and who act swiftly

We have loved our church culture too much. We have loved our churches too much. They will come and go, rise and fall, grow and die. What endures is the grace of God. What endures is the mission of God. God invites your congregation to mission. God encourages your congregation not to be the center of people's lives, but rather to be *in* the center of their lives.

May God give you compassion and peace, wisdom and judgment, common sense and prayer. My prayer is that the grace of God be with you in the days to come.

Hope is stronger than memory. Forgiveness is stronger than bitterness. Reconciliation is stronger than hatred. Light is stronger than darkness. Resurrection is stronger than crucifixion. The Open Tomb is stronger than the bloodied cross. The Risen Lord is stronger than the dead Jesus. Easter is stronger than Good Friday.

Hope is stronger than memory.

We are the Easter People. We are the People of Hope. We are the People of the Open Tomb, the Risen Lord, and New Life in Christ. We are the People of Mission. We are the People of Grace.

May the grace and peace of God bless you .... this day and forever more.

ACKNOWLEDGMENTS

I am deeply grateful to the thousands of leaders with whom I have had the privilege of sharing and working across the years. I am most appreciative of the thousands of pastors with whom I have shared and worked across the years. I am humbly thankful for the countless thousands upon thousands of grassroots persons with whom I have had the honor of working and sharing across the years.

I have learned much from key leaders. I have learned much from pastors. I have learned much from grassroots persons. All three groupings have contributed greatly to my understanding of momentum, resources, and strengths in congregations. This book is in honor of all of these key leaders, pastors, and grassroots persons.

The *Twelve Keys* books have lives of their own. They find their way to leaders, pastors, and congregations whom Julie and I will never have the pleasure of knowing personally.

It is amazing how helpful the *Twelve Keys* books are with congregations of all constituencies, shapes, and backgrounds—small, medium, large, mega, rural, small town, large city, and metropolitan—across the planet. Julie and I are grateful the *Twelve Keys* books help so many congregations.

As the books have traveled the planet, an extraordinary range of leaders, pastors, and congregations have been kind to share their excellent ideas and good suggestions. We are most humbly thankful to all of them. We have learned much. Further research and experience have come to pass.

I want to thank Jossey-Bass and the extraordinary team of persons gathered there: Sheryl Fullerton, executive editor; Debbie Notkin, contracts manager; Alison Knowles, senior editorial assistant; and Joanne Clapp Fullagar, editorial production manager. Each of them has given excellent wisdom and encouragement to this new work. I am grateful for their gifts, thoughtfulness, and insight.

This new book, *The Twelve Keys Leaders' Guide,* along with the new *Twelve Key to an Effective Church, Second Edition,* and *The Twelve Keys Bible Study,* join the *Twelve Keys* family of resources for congregations. I am grateful for the gifts and competencies with which the leadership team of Jossey-Bass has brought these three new books to publication.

I am grateful to our older son, Ken, who has been kind enough to create a new Web site, www.twelvekeys.org. There, you will discover helpful possibilities for seminars, speaking invitations, consulting resources, and *Twelve Keys* planning retreats. You will find ways to order the books and to register for major seminars I lead each year. You will discover wonderful pictures of our family.

I want to thank Julie for her love, wisdom, and major contributions. It is a rich experience to share and work with her in our life together.

Julie and I are most grateful for the wonderful persons across the planet with whom we are friends and family. God bless you all.

Kennon L. Callahan, Ph. D.

ABOUT THE AUTHOR

Kennon L. Callahan, B.A., M.Div., S.T.M., Ph.D., is grateful to be the husband of Julia McCoy Callahan, his best friend and beloved wife. An honored researcher, professor, and pastor, Dr. Callahan is today's most sought-after church consultant and speaker. Author of many books, he is best known for his groundbreaking *Twelve Keys to an Effective Church*, forming the widely acclaimed Mission Growth Movement, helping congregations across the planet.

Thousands of congregations and tens of thousands of church leaders and pastors around the world have been helped through his writings and workshops.

His seminars are filled with compassion, wisdom, encouragement, and practical possibilities.

He travels extensively, speaking to groups of pastors and key leaders from the United States, Canada, Australia, New Zealand, South Africa, and many other parts of the world.

An Ordained Elder in the United Methodist Church, Dr. Callahan taught for many years at Emory University. His fields of research and teaching include theology of mission, leadership and administration, and giving and finance.

Dr. Callahan is the founder of the Center for Continuing Education at Emory's Candler School of Theology. He is the founder of the National Certification Program in Church Finance and Administration, providing training and certification for pastors and church administrators. He has received many awards and recognitions, including being elected to the Hall of Fame of the National Association of Church Business Administrators.

Dr. Callahan is the founder and Senior Fellow of the National Institute for Church Planning and Consultation. Dr. Callahan is acclaimed as the founder of the Mission Growth Movement.

His pastoral experience spans rural and urban congregations in Ohio, Texas, and Georgia, and includes small, strong congregations, healthy middle congregations, and large, regional congregations.

Dr. Callahan has earned the B.A., M.Div., S.T.M., and Ph.D. degrees.

Bachelor of Arts, Kent State University, major in Philosophy, double minors in Religion and Psychology

Master of Divinity, Perkins School of Theology, Southern Methodist University, Systematic Theology, Historical Theology, and Sociology of Religion

Master of Sacred Theology, Perkins School of Theology, Theology of the Church and the Leadership and Administration of Congregations

Doctor of Philosophy, Emory University, Systematic Theology, the Nature and Mission of the Church

Dr. Callahan and his wife, Julia, have two sons and three grandchildren. They share a love of the outdoors, music, quilting, dogs, astronomy, reading, traveling, writing, geology, and sailing.

Twelve Keys to an Effective Church, Second Edition, Strong, Healthy Congregations Living in the Grace of God

The five basic qualities for strong, healthy congregations. Plus, new possibilities for the *Twelve Keys* to an effective, successful congregation. New suggestions for expanding your current strengths and adding new strengths. New wisdom and insights for mission, sacrament, and grace.

The Twelve Keys Leaders' Guide, An Approach for Grassroots, Key Leaders, and Pastors Together

Momentum. Resources. Strengths. The book helps you build the momentum of your congregation, deepen the resources of your congregation, and advance the strengths of your congregation. Your congregation will develop a strong, healthy future. The book shares excellent ideas and good suggestions on how to lead a helpful Twelve Keys Celebration Retreat. The book provides resources for encouraging momentum and action. It shares insights on the dynamics of memory, change, conflict, and hope. The book is an excellent companion for the new *Twelve Keys* book.

The Twelve Keys Bible Study

The book shares the Biblical resources for the **Twelve Keys**. It shares scriptures for each of the **Twelve Keys** and reflections on these scriptures. It shares suggestions and questions for study and conversation. This resource is helpful for Advent and Lenten Bible studies, Sunday School classes, small group studies, and for preaching and worship services. The book is an excellent companion Bible study for the new **Twelve Keys** book.

The Future That Has Come

The seven major paradigm shifts of recent years. New possibilities for reaching and growing the grassroots. Motivating and leading your congregation.

Small, Strong Congregations

Ministers, leaders, and members of small congregations develop a strong, healthy future together.

A New Beginning for Pastors and Congregations

What to do in the first three months of a new pastorate; how to make a new start in a present pastorate.

Preaching Grace

Pastors develop an approach to preaching that matches their own distinctive gifts.

Twelve Keys for Living

People claim the strengths God gives them and develop a whole, healthy life. Solid Lent or Advent study.

Visiting in an Age of Mission

Develop shepherding in your congregation. Groupings to shepherd. The variety of ways you can do so.

Effective Church Finances

Develop an effective budget, set solid giving goals, and increase the giving of your congregation.

Dynamic Worship

Major resources for stirring, inspiring worship services, helpful and hopeful in advancing people's lives.

Giving and Stewardship

How to grow generous givers. Motivations out of which people give. Six primary sources of giving. Giving Principles in generous congregations. How to encourage your whole giving family.

Effective Church Leadership

Foundational life searches. Seven best ways to grow leaders. Develop constructive leadership.

Building for Effective Mission

Develop your mission. Evaluate locations. Maximize current facilities. Building new space. Create an effective building team. Selecting an architect. Develop an extraordinary first year.

Twelve Keys to an Effective Church, Strategic Planning for Mission

Claim your current strengths, expand some, and add new strengths to be a strong, healthy congregation. Encourage your whole congregation to study this book—it helps in their church, family, work, and life.

Twelve Keys: The Planning Workbook

Each person contributes directly to creating an effective long-range plan for your future together.

Twelve Keys: The Leaders' Guide

How to lead your congregation in developing an effective plan for your future. How to develop action, implementation, and momentum. Dealing with the dynamics of memory, change, conflict, and hope.

Twelve Keys: The Study Guide

An excellent bible study of the *Twelve Keys,* with helpful resources and solid discussion possibilities.

INDEX

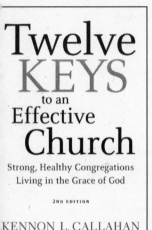

Twelve Keys to an Effective Church

Strong, Healthy Congregations Living in the Grace of God,
Second Edition

Kennon L. Callahan

ISBN 978-0-470-55929-1
Cloth | 288 pp.

New suggestions for expanding your current strengths and adding new strengths.

New wisdom and insights for mission, sacrament, and grace.

In this second edition of his groundbreaking book, Kennon Callahan identifies the twelve essential qualities of successful, growing churches and offers all congregations a way to unlock their potential for effective ministry. The Twelve Keys program balances practical planning with theological understanding to help churches function more effectively as they seek to grow and better serve their members.

KENNON L. CALLAHAN, PH.D. researcher, professor, and pastor is one of today's most sought-after church consultants. He has worked with thousands of congregations around the world and has helped tens of thousands of church leaders and pastors through his dynamic workshops and seminars. Author of many books, he is best known for his groundbreaking study *Twelve Keys to an Effective Church*, which has formed the basis for the Mission Growth Movement, a widely acclaimed program for church renewal.

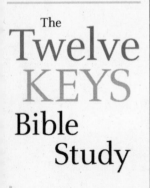

The Twelve Keys Bible Study

Kennon L. Callahan

ISBN 978-0-470-55916-1
Paper | 96 pp.

This resource is helpful for Advent and Lenten Bible studies, and for preaching and worship services.

An excellent companion Bible study for the new edition of ***Twelve Keys to an Effective Church***.

As a companion volume to *Twelve Keys to an Effective Church*, the Bible Study offers clergy and church leaders biblical resources for each of the twelve keys. This handy resource includes reflections on the scriptures as well as suggestions and questions for study and conversation that are suitable for individuals, groups, congregations, worship services, and retreats.

KENNON L. CALLAHAN, PH.D. researcher, professor, and pastor is one of today's most sought-after church consultants. He has worked with thousands of congregations around the world and has helped tens of thousands of church leaders and pastors through his dynamic workshops and seminars. Author of many books, he is best known for his groundbreaking study *Twelve Keys to an Effective Church*, which has formed the basis for the Mission Growth Movement, a widely acclaimed program for church renewal.